D1130992

# THE REGIONAL THEORY OF WORLD TRADE

# THE REGIONAL THEORY
# OF WORLD TRADE

## Andreas Grotewold
Slippery Rock State College

PTOLEMY PRESS, LTD.
Grove City, Pennsylvania

PTOLEMY PRESS, LTD.
P.O. Box 243
Grove City, Pennsylvania 16127

International Standard Book Number: 0-933550-00-6
Library of Congress Catalog Card Number: 79-83769

Printed in the United States of America by Globe
Printing Company, New Wilmington, Pennsylvania

To
RAYMOND E. MURPHY
who showed the way

and to
THE TAXPAYERS OF PENNSYLVANIA
who paid the fare

# CONTENTS

# FIGURES

# TABLES

# PREFACE

BEHIND EVERY THEORY there is a basically simple idea. Behind classical and neoclassical trade theory there is the principle of comparative advantage; behind Johann Heinrich von Thünen's theory is the idea that farmers maximize their land rent; behind Alfred Weber's theory is the notion that manufacturers minimize their transport and labor costs; behind central place theory is the recognition that the hierarchy of central places is related to a hierarchy of central goods and services; and behind the regional theory of world trade is the idea that regions which differ in their industrial structure differ in the trade which they generate.

Basic to the regional theory of world trade is the distinction between core areas and periphery, and the recognition that core areas are the nodal regions of world commerce. This was enunciated by Andreas Predöhl three decades ago; it is not a new idea. My contribution is a definition of core areas which serves to explain why they are the nodal regions of world commerce, why they generate a large volume of trade within and among themselves, and why the trade of the periphery is necessarily focused upon them. What Predöhl has stated as empirical laws can largely be deduced from my definition of core areas.

In international economics and international development

theory nations are the territorial units of concern. The regional theory departs from this point of view. Nonetheless, many of my inspirations derive from the works of international economists and development theorists. The relationship between intra- and interregional trade on the one hand, and international trade on the other, will become evident in the following pages.

Several friends have commented on an earlier draft of this study. They are George S. Quick and Paul N. Worthington of the Economics Department at Slippery Rock State College; James C. Hughes, Paul F. Rizza, and Peter W. Urbscheit of the Georgraphy Department at Slippery Rock State College; and Ulv Masing of the Geography Department at Edinboro State College. In response to their comments I have expanded several sections of my text and formulated my ideas more fully and precisely. I am very grateful for their help.

The library of Slippery Rock State College is a model of competence and efficiency. Its reference and bibliographical sections are good. Much of what I desired sat on its shelves, and any additional requests were answered promptly. Many thanks to its staff from a client well served.

Before this book was completed I contributed a paper, "The Industrialization of Peripheral Regions and the Patterns of World Trade," to a special issue of *Die Erde* in commemoration of the 150th anniversary of the Gesellschaft für Erdkunde zu Berlin. In the present book, Chapter 4 and part of Chapter 5 cover the same ground. Thanks are due to the Gesellschaft für Erdkunde zu Berlin for permitting me to repeat my own words with minor changes.

# 1

# INTRODUCTION

THE REGIONAL THEORY OF WORLD TRADE is concerned with types
of trade between and within types of regions. The regions are
not coincident with national territories. Two types of regions
are being distinguished: core areas (of which there are
several), and a vast, undifferentiated periphery. Chapter 2
deals with that distinction. The third chapter relates the
geographic pattern of core areas and periphery to the flow of
commodities, or the flow of commodities to the pattern of core
areas and periphery. It demonstrates that the volume and
commodity composition of international trade is largely
explained by the underlying pattern of core areas and
periphery. The fourth chapter examines the geographic
pattern of economic development. Specifically, it attributes
the poverty which prevails in many peripheral regions to an
imbalance of core areas and periphery, and anticipates future
changes in the regional structure of the world economy. The
fifth and last chapter acknowledges limitations of the regional
theory in its present state and raises critical issues in the
design of commercial and development policies — issues to
which no current theory offers a solution but which, given
appropriate empirical research, are more likely resolved by
the regional theory than by any other thus far proposed.
  The purpose of this introductory chapter is to relate the

regional theory of world trade to neoclassical trade theory and the factor proportions theorem. Readers who do not wish to pursue this discourse may move on directly to Chapter 2.

The regional theory may be considered an extension of neoclassical trade theory and of industrial location theory. Neoclassical trade theory is based on the principle of comparative advantage.[1] The principle asserts that trade takes place in response to regional or national differences in relative prices. A relative price is the price of one commodity in terms of another. Suppose, for example, that in Portugal a bolt of cloth fetches more wine than in England, and that in England a cask of wine fetches more cloth than in Portugal. In this situation a merchant can obtain more wine for his cloth if he sells the cloth in Portugal, and he can obtain more cloth for his wine if he sells the wine in England. Because of the difference in relative prices, Portugal has a comparative advantage in wine and exports wine to England, whereas England has a comparative advantage in cloth and exports cloth to Portugal. The regional theory takes geographic differences in relative prices for granted. It draws upon industrial location theory for criteria by which to distinguish core areas from periphery, and demonstrates that those two types of regions have comparative advantages in different types of goods.

In terms of potential applications the regional theory competes with the factor proportions theorem — often called Heckscher-Ohlin theorem.[2] The theorem asserts that regions or countries specialize in the production of goods requiring large inputs of their most abundant and relatively cheap

1. Gottfried Haberler, *A Survey of International Trade Theory*, rev. ed., Special Papers in International Economics No. 1 (Princeton, New Jersey: Princeton University, Department of Economics, International Finance Section. 1961).

2. For the authentic exposition of the theorem see Bertil Ohlin, *Interregional and International Trade*, rev. ed. (Cambridge, Massachusetts: Harvard University Press, 1967).

factor of production, and small inputs of their scarcest and relatively dear factor of production. Thus, densely settled Hong Kong might be expected to export labor intensive goods such as textiles, apparel, and electronic components, whereas Australia with her wide open spaces might be expected to export land intensive commodities such as wool, mutton, grains, or minerals. Ohlin has stated:

> In brief, commodities containing a large proportion of dear factors are imported, and those containing a large proportion of cheap factors are exported.[3]

At first glance this appears to be a plausible explanation of the commodity composition of interregional and international trade. Nonetheless, as one attempts to apply the factor proportions theorem to concrete situations, one encounters various complications.

In the first place, the proportions in which factors of production are being used to produce a given good are not identical everywhere. Both Thailand and the United States, for example, are exporters of rice, but in the growing of rice factors are used in different proportions in the two countries. In Thailand rice is a labor intensive crop by American standards, whereas in the United States rice is a capital intensive crop by Thai standards. The factor proportions theorem, however, cannot accommodate such differences in the techniques of production. If it did, it might lead one to the absurd conclusion that the United States imported labor intensive rice from Thailand, and that Thailand imported capital intensive rice from the United States. Or it might lead one to the conclusion that the United States as well as Thailand exported rice to a third country, which might be Japan. Suppose that the capital/labor ratio in the United States were 3:1. in Japan 2:1, and in Thailand 1:1. This supposition might imply that Japan imported capital intensive rice from the relatively capital abundant United States, and labor

3. Ibid., p. 19.

intensive rice from the relatively labor abundant Thailand. But it might imply also that Japan exported labor intensive rice to the relatively labor scarce United States, and capital intensive rice to the relatively capital scarce Thailand.

This example demonstrates that the factor proportions theorem, if it admitted interregional or international differences in production techniques, could not be used to predict which country exported rice and which country imported rice, or any other specific commodity.[4] Therefore, the factor proportions theorem must necessarily stipulate that production techniques be the same everywhere. This is justified by two propositions: (1) trade tends to equalize factor prices among regions, and (2) given equivalent, or nearly equivalent, factor prices everywhere, techniques of production for the same goods would be identical also.[5] Applied to our example, trade in rice would tend to increase wages in Thailand relative to the United States, and raise land rents in the United States relative to Thailand. Eventually, when factor prices had come to be equivalent, or nearly equivalent, the techniques of producing rice would no longer differ significantly between the two countries.

The theoretical validity of the first proposition — that is, the factor price equalization theorem — has been demonstrated, but the premises underlying the proof are unrealistic.[6] A confirmation of the empirical relevance of the factor price equalization theorem under current circumstances seems most unlikely. Government regulation of foreign trade is pervasive and in many cases specifically aimed at preventing an equalization of factor prices — especially wages. Any restraint upon international factor price equalization, of

4. This argument is developed more fully in J. L. Ford, "The Ohlin-Heckscher Theory of the Basis of Commodity Trade," *Economic Journal*, Vol. 73 (September 1963), pp. 458-476.

5. Ohlin, *Interregional and International Trade*, pp. 8-9 and 24-28. For qualifications and exceptions see pp. 64-72.

6. See Paul A. Samuelson, "International Trade and the Equalisation of Factor Prices," *Economic Journal*, Vol. 58 (June 1948), pp. 163-184; and idem, "International Factor Equalisation Once Again," ibid:, Vol. 59 (June 1949), pp. 181-197.

course, undermines the factor proportions theorem. In an appendix to the second edition of his *Interregional and International Trade* Ohlin has acknowledged this explicitly.[7]

A second flaw of the factor proportions theorem is its failure to recognize that a region's export commodities are not necessarily products of that region. Exports of manufactured goods may have a significant import component. Both Venezuela and the Netherlands, for instance, are exporters of petroleum products. Venezuela's exports, made from domestic crude oil, are products of Venezuelan land as well as capital and labor. The Netherlands' exports of petroleum products, on the other hand, are made from imported crude oil. They are products of Dutch capital and labor, but the domestic land component is missing. This is not an isolated, peculiar, or exceptional case. If, as in an input-output study, the input requirements of the manufactured goods traded internationally were traced to their origin, it would almost certainly appear (1) that many exports of manufactured goods have a more than negligible import component, and (2) that the import component of the exports of the United States is smaller than the import component of the manufactured exports of Canada, the west European countries, and Japan.

Third, it must be recognized that the presence of factors of production does not necessarily entail their use.[8] Of two regions with equal endowments of capital relative to labor, one may nonetheless be relatively capital scarce if its capital goods are used only eight hours a day and if the other region's capital goods are used twenty-four hours a day.

Fourth, in some regions a relative abundance of certain factors may be more than offset by a relatively large demand for the products of these same factors.[9] Great Britain, for example, has extensive pastures for sheep grazing; none-

7. Ohlin, *Interregional and International Trade*, pp. 310-311.

8. Noted in Jacob Viner, "Relative Abundance of the Factors and International Trade," *Indian Economic Journal*, Vol. 9 (January 1962), pp. 274-288, reference to p. 287.

9. Ibid., p. 277.

theless, she is a substantial importer of mutton and wool — partly because of the dietary habits of her people, and partly because of her large woolen textile industry. The factor proportions theorem does not ignore demand; but, as in the following quotation, it is ambivalent in recognizing demand as a determinant of trade.

> As a matter of fact, little attention need be given to the theoretical possibility of two isolated regions having the same relative commodity prices, in which case no interregional trade could arise. Unless there is in a given case some special reason for the opposite supposition, one is justified in assuming that conditions of supply of factors and demand are such that the relative scarcity will be different in the two regions in an isolated state — differences in supply being probably as a rule more important than differences in demand. In a loose sense, therefore, differences in equipment of factors of production will be the cause of trade. But one must be careful to remember the qualification implicit in the possible influence of differences in demand conditions, for the ultimate determinant of interregional trade, as of all price phenomena, is the relation between the factor supply and the demand conditions.[10]

Last, but not least, many a country exports as well as imports goods which incorporate virtually identical factors of production in virtually identical proportions. Consider the exchange of passenger cars among the countries of Western Europe. Many Italian Fiat cars are owned in France and West Germany, French Renault cars are popular in West Germany and Italy, and German Volkswagen are common in Italy and France. Although these types of cars are not quite identical, they all are made in manufacturing plants where factors of production are employed in roughly similar proportions. There is, of course, a rational explanation for this trade, to

---

10. Ohlin, *Interregional and International Trade*, p. 10.

which we shall turn later. What matters in this discourse is that such trade cannot be explained by the factor proportions theorem.

These comments are not meant to be an indiscriminate rejection of the factor proportions theorem, but they suggest that the theorem has serious flaws and limitations. The regional theory of world trade has limitations also. These will be noted in the last chapter, after the content of the theory has been presented.

# 2
# CORE AREAS AND PERIPHERY

THE MODERN WORLD ECONOMY has evolved concomitantly with the Industrial Revolution.[1] During the late eighteenth and early nineteenth centuries Great Britain became the focal region, or core area, of a unicentric world economy. Other inhabited lands came to comprise the periphery. After the Napoleonic wars the Industrial Revolution spread to the European continent. Thus a European core area was created. Fifty years later, after the Civil War in the United States, a second core area came into existence in eastern North America. This established a bicentric world economy.

The commerce of the European and North American core areas expanded vigorously during the half century prior to World War I, when it gave rise to the development of large peripheral regions. Into this period fall the development of livestock ranching and grain farming in the former Louisiana Territory and the Argentine Pampas, the modernization of the sugar industry in Cuba, the rapid increase in coffee cultivation in Brazil, the nitrate boom and the beginnings of the modern copper industry in Chile, the development of iron mining in the arctic lands of northern Sweden, the growth of cotton cultivation in Egypt, the beginnings of cocoa production

---

1. Andreas Predöhl, *Aussenwirtschaft,* 2nd ed. (Göttingen: Vandenhoeck und Ruprecht, 1971), pp. 67-149.

in West Africa, the growth of the jute industry in Bengal, the first tea exports from Sri Lanka, and the development of rubber plantations and tin mines in Southeast Asia. This expansive phase before World War I has had a profound impact on the regional structure of the world economy which is discernible to this day.

Today we think in terms of a multicentric world economy. Thus far, two additional core areas have come into existence: one in the Soviet Union, the other in Japan. And more core areas are developing elsewhere.

The distinction between core areas and periphery is fundamental to the regional theory of world trade, because trade flows are explained on the basis of this dichotomy. In the next chapter we shall demonstrate that core areas are the focal regions of world commerce. Core areas generate a large volume of trade within and among themselves, and they are the major markets for periphery exports as well as the chief sources of periphery imports.

This chapter deals with the distinction between core areas and the periphery. By itself, it may be considered a contribution to the question of economic regionalization. But that is not its main purpose. Regionalization is useful only in a given context[2] — and our context, of course, is the regional theory of world trade.

## Definition of Core Areas

A core area is characterized by a complex of vertically

2. On the value of regionalization we agree with Richard Hartshorne. He has argued that any definition and delineation of regions necessarily and properly depends on the purpose of the study; that regional divisions are useful only for the purpose of a particular study; and that by themselves they cannot be considered a contribution to knowledge. *Perspective on the Nature of Geography* (Chicago: Rand McNally for the Association of American Geographers, 1959), pp. 129-145.

integrated manufacturing industries.[3] Associated with such a complex are a wide range of specialized technological, construction, transportation, and administrative services. We recognize that such services are an inseparable adjunct to a manufacturing complex; but in defining and delineating core areas the service industries need not be taken into account.

Peripheral regions have manufacturing industries also. The difference between core areas and periphery is that the former contain manufacturing industries which are vertically integrated with each other, whereas the latter's manufacturing industries are not.

Concrete examples may help to clarify the distinction between core areas and periphery. Typical of core industries is the complex of automotive factories centered on the Detroit-Windsor area. Many plants in this complex use intermediate goods (metals, plastics, etc.) to make more highly fabricated intermediate goods (parts and accessories of automobiles). They have backward linkages, forward linkages, or both types of linkages within the manufacturing sector of their own region.

Compare the Detroit-Windsor area with a peripheral manufacturing center such as Kansas City whose leading industries are meat packing plants, flour mills, petroleum refineries, an automobile assembly plant, and a steel mill. These do not constitute an integrated complex, because there are no important linkages among them. True, the oil refineries send some fuel oil to the steel mill, and the steel mill sends nuts and bolts to the automobile assembly plant. Virtually all of the parts and accessories used in Kansas City's automobile assembly plant, however, are received from within 400 km or so of Detroit. The output of Kansas City's steel mill consists mostly of nails, rods, bars, and welded fabric for the local

---

3. According to Predöhl the development of core areas (Kerngebiete or Industriekerne) begins with the growth of agglomerative (raumbildende) industries, especially with the growth of the iron and steel industry. Aussenwirtschaft, pp. 73-149. I have registered objections in "The Growth of Industrial Core Areas and Patterns of World Trade," Annals of the Association of American Geographers, Vol. 61 (June 1971), pp. 361-370.

construction industry, and of barbed wire for use on farms and ranches in Kansas City's extensive rural trade area. Kansas City's petroleum ref.neries receive crude oil from Texas and Oklahoma. Their chief products are gasoline, jet fuel, distillate fuel for home and office heating, heavy residual oil for industrial heating, and asphalt. Their major market is the local service sector, including the Kansas City airport. Light hydrocarbon gas, a basic material for antifreeze and other products, is burned in the refining process, because it has no market in the Kansas City area and cannot be shipped economically to distant places. The meat packing plants and flour mills process raw materials from Kansas City's trade area.

If any of Kansas City's manufacturing industries ceased to exist, the others would hardly be affected. The relationships which do exist among Kansas City's manufacturing industries are mostly indirect. Jointly they make it worthwhile to provide an infrastructure of transportation and commercial services for the Kansas City region. Moreover, the labor force of each factory constitutes a local market for the products of all the others. Such indirect relationships are not at all comparable to the direct linkages within the manufacturing sector of core areas.

The comparison of the Detroit-Windsor area with Kansas City helps us to recognize the difference between core areas and peripheral manufacturing centers, but is of no help in establishing a geographic boundary between them. The delineation of core areas is made difficult by the fact that many manufacturing industries typical of core areas have forward or backward linkages to manufacturing industries found in peripheral regions — forward linkages, for example, to automobile assembly plants in Kansas City, Mexico, or South Africa, and backward linkages to copper smelters in Arizona or Chile. In other words, it may well be argued that the complex of vertically integrated manufacturing industries, which we said was characteristic of core areas, extends world-wide.

To separate regions which contain a complex of vertically integrated manufacturing industries from those which do not, we must distinguish between peripheral and core industries. Core areas, then, may be defined as regions where core industries are concentrated. But peripheral industries — such as oil refineries, automobile assembly plants, meat packing plants, breweries, and many others — may occur in peripheral regions as well as in core areas.

The criteria for distinguishing between peripheral and core industries are suggested by industrial location theory in Alfred Weber's original formulation.[4] According to Weber manufacturing plants are agents in a productive process which transforms raw materials through one or several stages of manufacturing into finished goods. The terms *raw* material and *finished* good are used in their literal meaning. *Raw* materials are synonymous with primary products. This implies, for instance, that a chemical plant located on the Texas Gulf Coast because of easy access to intermediate and by-products of nearby oil refineries cannot be classified as a raw material-oriented industry. According to Weber the location of such a plant is explained by agglomerative economies.[5] Its material supplies are intermediate goods, not raw materials. By the same token, *finished* goods include only products which are not subject to further manufacturing and which in their current state do not become part of another manufactured good. They comprise consumer goods as well as capital equipment, including capital equipment for the manufacturing sector. Also, they include manufactured supplies to be used up by the primary and service sectors (such as fertilizer and building materials, respectively). *Intermediate* goods, of course, are manufactured supplies (as distinguished from capital equipment) which do become part of another manufactured good or are subject to further

---

4. Alfred Weber, *Theory of the Location of Industries*, trans. Carl J. Friedrich (Chicago: University of Chicago Press, 1929).

5. Ibid., p. 205.

manufacturing. What follows makes sense only if we apply this terminology consistently.

According to Weber the location of manufacturing industries is explained by either "transport-orientation," labor-orientation, or agglomerative economies. "Transport-oriented" industries, according to Weber, are drawn either to the sources of their raw materials or power, or to the markets for their finished products. This implies that industries drawn to their suppliers of intermediate goods, or to the customers for their intermediate products, are located where they are because of agglomerative economies. Such industries are not "transport-oriented" according to Weber.

Weber's restrictive use of the term "transport-oriented" is confusing. Producers of intermediate goods drawn to their customers, or factories drawn to their suppliers of intermediate goods, are affected by transport economies as well as by agglomerative economies. To classify such industries as agglomerative and to exclude them from *transport-oriented* industries (in the literal sense of that term) makes no sense. Transport economies and agglomerative economies are not mutually exclusive.

Despite its confusing terminology — and other short-comings as well[6] — it was Weber's theory which has suggested to me how to distinguish between core and peripheral industries. In the first place, I accept Weber's distinction between raw materials, intermediate products, and finished goods, as explained above. Second, I disaggregate the market for finished goods into a market for consumer goods, a market for manufactured supplies for the primary and service sectors, and a market for capital goods. Third, the market for capital

6. According to Weber manufacturers seek out the least cost location, whereas we suppose that they seek out the most profitable location. We agree with August Lösch who has criticized that "Weber's solution for the problem of location proves to be incorrect as soon as not only cost but also sales possibilities are considered. His fundamental error consists in seeking the place of lowest cost. This is as absurd as to consider the point of largest sales as the proper location. Every such one-sided orientation is wrong." *The Economics of Location*, trans. William H. Woglom and Wolfgang F. Stolper (New York: John Wiley and Sons, 1967), pp. 28-29.

goods has to be disaggregated further into customers in the primary, manufacturing, and service sectors. Fourth, I distinguish between low-wage, relatively unskilled labor on the one hand, and more highly paid professional, technical, and skilled labor on the other.

Peripheral industries, then, belong to the following three types:

1. Factories whose dominant location factor is proximity to their major raw materials or sources of power.
2. Factories producing finished goods other than capital goods for the manufacturing sector whose dominant location factor is proximity to their customers.
3. Factories whose dominant location factor is the availability of low-wage labor.

Core industries — those comprising a complex of vertically integrated manufacturing industries — can be classified into two types:

1. Factories whose dominant location factor is proximity to other factories — regardless whether they are joined by backward or forward linkages, and regardless whether shipments between them consist of intermediate or capital goods.
2. Factories whose dominant location factor is the availability of professional, technical, and skilled labor.

This classification of manufacturing industries by their locational characteristics differs in principle from the customary classification of industries by their products. There is no certain way of relating our classification to the Standard Industrial Classification of the U.S. Bureau of the Census, or to the International Standard Industrial Classification of the United Nations Statistical Office. Steel mills, for example, may be core or peripheral industries. A comparison of two ARMCO steel plants — the one in Kansas City, the other in Butler, Pennsylvania — demonstrates this point. As can be inferred from earlier remarks, the Kansas City plant belongs to the second type of peripheral industry; it is a producer of finished goods (not subject to further manufacturing) for the primary and service sectors, and its dominant location factor is proximity to its customers. The Butler plant, on the other hand, is a core industry. Its dominant location factor is proximity to other manufacturing plants, with which it is connected through both backward and forward linkages. Its major inputs are pig iron and ingot mold scrap. These come from yet another ARMCO plant in Ashland, Kentucky, and additional specialty scrap is obtained through scrap brokers. The Butler plant's chief product is electric grade steel of specific magnetic qualities for use in power and distribution transformers. All of the plant's outputs are intermediate products made to specifications of other manufacturers. Nearly two-thirds of the Butler plant's output is sent to other manufacturing plants in the northeastern United States and in southern Ontario.

Core areas are the chief centers of industrial inventions and innovations.[7] In the making of new products or in the application of new manufacturing processes easy access to engineering consultants, subcontractors who perform particular tasks, skilled labor, and suppliers who can provide specialized materials or equipment is necessary.

Products tend to pass through a life cycle. As this cycle takes its course, industries producing particular products

---

7. Edward L. Ullman, "Regional Development and the Geography of Concentration," *Papers and Proceedings of the Regional Science Association,* Vol. 4 (1958), pp. 179-198.

may change their locations.[8] Once the virtues of a new product have been demonstrated to its potential users, the demand for the product expands. The production process tends to become standardized, economies of large scale are being realized, and unit costs decline. Competitors are likely to enter the field, and the price of the product is reduced. Eventually, as a product comes of age, the industry manufacturing it is likely to shift its location. Three decades ago, for example, the manufacturing of black-and-white television receivers was a core industry based on technical and skilled labor; today it is a peripheral industry based on low-wage labor. Later the manufacturing of color television receivers went through the same cycle. Most recently the manufacturing of small computers passed also through the cycle. Many standardized electronic products are now made in the periphery — in countries such as South Korea, Taiwan, Hong Kong, and Singapore. But core areas continue to be the chief centers of industrial inventions and innovations.

Thus far we have dealt with the location of manufacturing industries in a competitive market. We have assumed that each factory selects its most profitable location. This, however, is not always true. On occasion, governments have intervened in location decisions, and cost considerations have been overruled by considerations of national security, the desire to prevent further congestion in regions of intensive urban development, or the wish to create new jobs in depressed areas or in parts of the periphery.[9] In some cases,

---

8. Raymond Vernon, "International Investment and International Trade in the Product Cycle," *Quarterly Journal of Economics*, Vol. 80 (May 1966), pp. 190-207; and Louis T. Wells, Jr., ed., *The Product Life Cycle and International Trade* (Boston: Harvard University, Graduate School of Business Administration, Division of Research, 1972).

9. Gerald Manners, "Regional Protection: A Factor in Economic Geography," *Economic Geography*, Vol. 38 (April 1962), pp. 122-129; and Robert C. Estall and Robert Ogilvie Buchanan, *Industrial Activity and Economic Geography — A Study of the Forces Behind the Geographical Location of Productive Activity in Manufacturing Industry*, rev. ed. (London: Hutchinson University Library, 1966), pp. 105-123.

core industries have been relegated to peripheral regions. Core industries thus displaced are geographically removed from the complex of integrated industries to which they are necessarily linked. Specific examples of displaced core industries will be cited after the existing core areas have been delineated.

## Delineation of Core Areas

As already noted, core areas contain core industries as well as peripheral industries. But core industries, by definition, do not belong within peripheral regions. Wherever they have become part of the industrial structure, core area growth has begun. Obviously, the existing core areas have not originated overnight. This suggests that there are regions in a stage of transition from peripheral manufacturing center to fully developed core area. The difference between core areas and the periphery, therefore, is one of degree, whereas the difference between core and peripheral industries is one of kind.

To separate core areas from the periphery, one must set apart regions which contain a significant assemblage of core industries as well as some peripheral industries from regions which contain mostly peripheral industries and only a few core industries or none at all. Deciding what constitutes a "significant" assemblage of core industries involves an element of judgment. Moreover, as mentioned above, core industries and peripheral industries are defined by their dominant location factors, whereas published statistics and maps show the distribution of industries classified by their products; and an industry's product is no certain indication of its dominant location factor. This implies that the separation of core areas from the periphery, if based on the available statistics and maps, inevitably involves inferences and guesses regarding the dominant location factors of industries in particular places. The following delineations have been derived with the help of such inferences and guesses. They are tentative and subject to revision on the basis of specific investigations.

Prior to World War II the European core area extended eastward as far as Szczecin and Prague. Presently the west European core area ends at the eastern border of West Germany and Austria. In the north it is bordered by Glasgow, Oslo, and Stockholm; its southern boundary is marked by Trieste, Bologna, and Marseille; and its western boundary extends from Marseille to Swansea, and then back to Glasgow.

The core industries of East Germany, Poland, and Czechoslovakia, which used to be part of the European core area, have severed their former connections at the insistence of the Soviet Union. The main purpose of Comecon or CMEA (Council for Mutual Economic Assistance) is to integrate these industries with the Soviet Union's economy. An integration of several centrally planned economies administered by more or less autonomous national governments, however, faces grave difficulties. The basic problem is that in centrally planned economies prices are determined by governments in accordance with their political objectives. Therefore the real costs of producing specific commodities are unknown.[10] Under such conditions the gains from trade are indeterminate, and each national government is apprehensive about making an unfavorable exchange.[11]

The North American core area extends from Portland, Maine, westward to Utica, Toronto, Port Huron, Bay City, Michigan, and Milwaukee; from there to Davenport and St.

10. Elisabeth L. Tamedly, *Socialism and International Economic Order* (Caldwell, Idaho: Caxton Printers, 1969), especially pp. 229-283.

11. For a thorough study of the methods of determining foreign trade prices among the CMEA membership and an analysis of their impact on the flow of trade see Edward A. Hewett, *Foreign Trade Prices in the Council for Mutual Economic Assistance* (New York: Cambridge University Press, 1974).

Louis; and then eastward to Cincinnati and Baltimore.[12] In terms of area it is only three-fifths the size of the west European core area. Politics, no doubt, has played a part in this. In Europe a dozen or so national governments could offer tariff protection to core industries located beyond the most favored manufacturing regions. In North America only two national governments have had this option. This is not to say that State or Provincial governments in North America have made no effort to attract core industries to peripheral locations, or that their efforts have been without results. It does suggest, however, that in the past the many sovereign national governments of Europe have been more effective in dispersing core industries, and that their ability to impose protective tariffs has been a major factor in their success. Only recently has the adoption of a common external tariff by the members of the European Communities (EC) restricted the power of national governments in this respect.

In the Soviet Union core industries have been spread over an even wider area in accordance with the central government's successive Five Year Plans. In my judgment the Soviet Union's core area extends over the territory framed by Rybinsk, Perm, Kamensk-Ural'skiy, Chelyabinsk, Magnitogorsk, Volgograd, Armavir, Krasnodar, Odessa, and Kiev.[13] Thus defined, it occupies a space roughly one and one-half times the size of the west European core area. As might be expected, such a dispersal of core industries entails a loss of final product either because of increased transport costs or because of reduced benefits from specialization among

---

12. This delineation coincides with the one proposed by Ullman in "Regional Development and the Geography of Concentration," p. 181. But Ullman's criterion for delineating this region is not specified.

13. Chauncy D. Harris has spoken of a "European industrial core of the Soviet Union from Moscow east to the Urals and south to the Black Sea and the North Caucasus." *Cities of the Soviet Union — Studies in Their Functions, Size, Density, and Growth,* Association of American Geographers Monograph No. 5 (Chicago: Rand McNally, 1970), p. 91. But what exactly is meant by "industrial core" is not clear.

factories.[14] The formidable respect which the Soviet Union's core area commands rests largely on its production of heavy machinery and armaments.

The Japanese core area, by contrast, is extremely compact and congested. It forms a narrow belt which stretches from Hitachi along the Pacific and Inland Sea coasts, and then across northern Kyushu to Nagasaki. Its farthest inland city is Maebashi, only 100 km or so from the Pacific shore.

Each of the four core areas named above possesses the facilities to create a great variety of intricate and technologically advanced products. Jointly they account for three percent of the world's inhabited lands, approximately twelve percent of the world's population, and an estimated 45 percent of the world's gross product (Figure 1).

Several other manufacturing regions have a lesser, yet impressive assemblage of core industries. Among them are the Bengal-Bihar-Orissa region of India, northeastern China, and southeastern Brazil. Incipient core areas exist in southern California, in southern Louisiana and eastern Texas, as well as in Mexico, Argentina, Israel, South Africa, the Bombay-Poona region of India, and in southeastern Australia.

Existing core areas may expand areally. In the past several decades the North American core area has expanded westward to Davenport - Rock Island - Moline with the growth of the agricultural machinery industry, and to St.

---

14. A decade or so ago 57 percent of the Soviet Union's machine building plants produced their own nonferrous castings, 71 percent made their own iron castings, and 84 percent produced their own forgings. In the United States, by comparison, only two percent of the machine building plants had their own casting shop, and only one percent had their own forging shop. Jozef Wilczynski, *Technology in Comecon — Acceleration of Technological Progress through Economic Planning and the Market* (New York: Praeger, 1974), pp. 291-292, citing *Voposy economiki,* August 1971, p. 102. Reduced benefits from specialization, or plant autarky, however, may result not only from industrial dispersal, but may occur also in response to incentives set in the course of national planning. See Tamedly, *Socialism and International Economic Order,* p. 238.

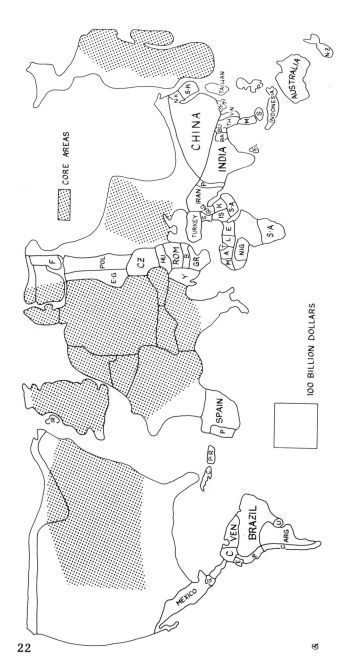

Figure 1 — Countries, core areas, and the periphery proportional to their gross domestic product in 1973. Some countries' product was too small to be distinguished on a graph at this scale.

Louis with the growth of the aircraft industry. In the future it may come to include Minneapolis - St. Paul in the northwest, Montreal in the northeast, and Louisville, Kentucky, in the South. The west European core area may come to include southwestern France, northeastern Spain, and eastern and southern Ireland.

In many instances the growth of core industries outside established core areas has been fostered by national governments. Thus, the beginning of the aircraft industry at Toulouse dates from World War I when the Latécoère Company moved there from the north to build reconnaissance planes at a safe distance from the front.[15] During the 1930s the aircraft engine company of Turboméca set up production facilities in Bordes, and government restrictions on industrial expansion in the Paris region led to the establishment of aircraft factories in Bayonne and Bordeaux. In the United States during World War II, a Boeing aircraft factory was established in Wichita, Kansas, for strategic reasons at the request of the Federal government. Also during World War II, the Federal government commissioned the United States Steel Corporation to build an integrated steel mill in Geneva, Utah, to supply shipyards and other steel using industries on the Pacific coast. The steel mill was built for the Federal government at a cost of $200 million, but after the war it was sold to the United States Steel Corporation for only $47.5 million — a striking example of loss attributable to an uneconomical location. Many other instances of government sponsored displacements of core industries could be cited, such as the spacecraft centers near Houston, Texas, and Huntsville, Alabama; the nuclear research and engineering facilities in Oak Ridge, Tennessee; and the Soviet Union's ordnance and machine building industry east of the Ural Mountains.

In many older industrial districts a further expansion of manufacturing activities is inhibited by traffic congestion,

15. David Ian Scargill, *Economic Geography of France* (New York: St. Martin's Press, 1968), p. 90.

public restrictions on air and water pollution, and high taxes to finance rehabilitation and modernization projects. Some core industries whose inputs and outputs are of high value per unit of weight and bulk have been able to evade these problems by establishing operations in remote peripheral locations. This, for instance, accounts for the presence of chemical and pharmaceutical factories in the tax-free zones of Bermuda and the Bahamas. Their products are shipped mostly by air, and they exist in symbiosis with the local tourist industry which also is dependent on air transport.

## Summary

A core area comprises a complex of vertically integrated manufacturing industries. The periphery has manufacturing industries too, but these have few if any backward or forward linkages with each other and therefore do not constitute a vertically integrated complex. If any peripheral industry ceased to exist, the others would hardly be affected.

The delineation of core areas is based on a distinction between core and peripheral industries; and this distinction, in turn, is based on a classification of manufacturing industries by their dominant location factors. The difference between core and peripheral industries is one of kind. The difference between core areas and the periphery, however, is one of degree. Some regions are in a stage of transition from peripheral manufacturing centers to fully developed core areas. Once fully developed, core areas possess the facilities to create a great variety of intricate and technologically advanced products. They are the chief centers of industrial inventions and innovations.

Presently the world economy is dominated by the core areas of Western Europe, North America, the Soviet Union, and Japan. The next chapter will demonstrate the relationship between their industrial structure and their significance in world trade.

# 3

# PATTERNS OF WORLD TRADE

CORE AREAS AND THE PERIPHERY differ in the trade which they
generate. Statistics of international trade conceal this
difference to some extent, because the boundaries of core
areas and nations do not usually coincide. Several nations —
notably the United States, Canada, France, Norway, Sweden,
Italy, the Soviet Union, and Japan — include sections of core
areas as well as periphery (Figure 1).

To relate the available international trade statistics to our
scheme of core areas and periphery, we shall distinguish
between core countries and peripheral countries. The former
are those which occupy a section of the west European or
North American core areas, as well as Japan. These same
countries are designated the "industrial countries" by the
International Monetary Fund.[1] Countries not so classified,

---

1. This coincidence is largely fortuitous. The IMF's distinction is based on
two criteria: (1) per capita gross national product, and (2) the ratio of the
product of manufacturing to the product of agriculture. (Personal letter from
Dr. Werner Dannemann, Director of the Bureau of Statistics, IMF.)
Presumedly every country designated "industrial" by the IMF outranks all
other countries in at least one of these criteria. The IMF's criteria, however,
bear no logically compelling relation to our distinction between core and
peripheral countries. It is conceivable that a peripheral country achieves a
high per capita gross national product, has a small agricultural sector, and a
relatively large sector of (chiefly peripheral) manufacturing industries. Hong
Kong, for instance, might possibly attain this status. If so, it would qualify as
an "industrial country" by the criteria of the IMF, but not as a core country by
our criterion.

however, have industries also; they are not "nonindustrial" by any conventional interpretation of that generally ambiguous term.[2] It seems preferable, therefore, to speak of core countries and peripheral countries.

The centrally planned economies we shall treat as a single unit — that is, consider their trade with the market economies, but not the trade among them. This is necessary for two reasons: (1) In the trade among centrally planned economies exchange rates are fixed and stable, and the prices of commodities are negoitated by state trading agencies with reference to those rigid exchange rates. The prices thus assigned to commodities may vary substantially from the prices of comparable commodities traded by market economies. In other words, the two sets of trade statistics — those of the market economies and those of the centrally planned economies — are not comparable. (2) The centrally planned economies' trade statistics are incomplete. Their trade by commodities does not always add up to their total trade.[3] The commodity compostion of their trade with the market economies can be inferred from the trade statistics published for the market economies; but the commodity composition of the trade among centrally planned economies is only imperfectly known. The centrally planned economies include the Soviet Union, Poland, East Germany, Czechoslovakia, Hungary, Romania, Bulgaria, Albania, China, the communist-controlled parts of former Indochina, and Cuba.

For documentation I have chosen trade statistics for the year 1973. It may be recalled that in December 1973 a sudden,

2. There are, of course, many industries outside the manufacturing sector — such as the mining industry which belongs to the primary sector, and the transport industry which belongs to the service sector. Even if the term "industry" were restricted to manufacturing activities — as in industrial as opposed to agricultural location theory — the peripheral countries could not be termed "nonindustrial," because they have manufacturing industries also.

3. According to a study by Barry L. Kostinsky, the residual consists of complete plants, some machinery and equipment, and other items. *Description and Analysis of Soviet Foreign Trade Statistics*, Foreign Economic Report No. 5 (Washington, D.C.: U.S. Department of Commerce, 1974).

steep increase in oil prices was imposed by OPEC (Organization of Petroleum Exporting Countries). Subsequently the prices of most other goods have increased also, but the rate of increase has been unequal for different commodities. The trade statistics for the next several years reflect this lack of equilibrium, which has caused more concern than usual over countries' terms of trade and balance of payments. At the time of this writing it appears that a new equilibrium in world trade will soon be established. But a comprehensive set of trade statistics reflecting the new equilibrium will not become available until several years hence.

Now we are ready to demonstrate how the patterns of international trade relate to our model of core areas and periphery.

## *Direction of International Trade*

In 1973 the world's total international trade valued f.o.b., excluding trade among the centrally planned economies, was $531 billion (Table 1, last row, last column). Of that total, $241 billion, or 45 percent, consisted of exports from the west European core countries (first row, last column of Table 1). And of that, in turn, nearly $150 billion, or 62 percent, consisted of shipments to each other (first row, first column of Table 1). Obviously, where a complex of vertically integrated manufacturing industries is overlaid by a multitude of national boundaries, a large volume of trade must necessarily pass over them. The explanation why countries which occupy sections of the same core area carry on a large volume of trade with each other is implicit in our definition of core areas.

In 1973 the total imports of the west European core countries amounted to nearly $241 billion (last row, first column of Table 1), whereas those of the United States and Canada amounted to only $90 billion (last row, sum of the second and third columns). The chief reason for this difference is political, or course. In the first place, the North American core area was shared by only two countries, whereas the west

## Table 1
## Direction of Trade, by Groups of Countries: 1973
### (In Millions of Current U.S. Dollars, F.O.B.)

| From: \ To: | West European Core Countries [a] | United States | Canada | Japan | Centrally Planned Economies [b] | Developed Peripheral Countries [c] | Oil Exporting Countries [d] | Poor Peripheral Countries [e] | World [f] |
|---|---|---|---|---|---|---|---|---|---|
| West European Core Countries [a] | 149,604 | 17,584 | 2,808 | 3,492 | 12,078 | 22,588 | 9,337 | 23,483 | 240,974 |
| United States | 18,504 | — | 15,104 | 8,313 | 2,492 | 4,965 | 3,806 | 17,486 | 70,670 |
| Canada | 3,460 | 17,116 | — | 1,800 | 764 | 539 | 293 | 1,230 | 25,202 |
| Japan | 5,433 | 9,573 | 1,002 | — | 2,066 | 3,096 | 2,821 | 11,426 | 35,417 |
| Centrally Planned Economies [b] | 10,163 | 611 | 209 | 2,244 | — | 2,443 | 1,060 | 3,438 | 20,168 |
| Developed Peripheral Countries [c] | 15,085 | 3,516 | 589 | 4,019 | 2,595 | 2,311 | 896 | 4,320 | 33,331 |
| Oil Exporting Countries [d] | 18,610 | 5,279 | 939 | 6,693 | 447 | 2,249 | 695 | 6,251 | 41,163 |
| Poor Peripheral Countries [e] | 19,906 | 14,531 | 1,085 | 7,619 | 3,380 | 3,528 | 2,406 | 11,709 | 64,164 |
| World [f] | 240,765 | 68,210 | 21,736 | 34,180 | 23,822 | 41,719 | 21,314 | 79,343 | 531,089 |

a Austria, Belgium-Luxembourg, Denmark, France, West Germany, Italy, the Netherlands, Norway, Sweden, Switzerland, and the United Kingdom.

b Albania, Bulgaria, China, Cuba, Czechoslovakia, East Germany, Hungary, the Mongolian Republic, North Korea, North Viet Nam, Poland, Romania, and the Soviet Union.

c Australia, the Faeroe Islands, Finland, Gibraltar, Greece, Iceland, Ireland, Malta, New Zealand, Portugal, South Africa, Spain, and Yugoslavia.

d Algeria, Bahrain, Brunei, Ecuador, Gabon, Indonesia, Iran, Iraq, Kuwait, Libya, Nigeria, Oman, Quatar, Saudi Arabia, Trinidad and Tobago, the United Arab Emirates, and Venezuela.

e All countries not specified elsewhere in the stub.

f Excludes shipments not specified by destination.

Sources: Direction of Trade: Annual 1970-74 (Washington, D.C.: International Monetary Fund and International Bank for Reconstruction and Development, no date). Statistics of the trade between West and East Germany were supplied by the German American Chamber of Commerce in New York.

European core area was shared by eleven countries (counting Belgium-Luxembourg as one). In economic terms the trade of New Jersey might reasonably be compared with that of the Netherlands; but for political reasons the Netherlands' trade with her neighbors was counted as international trade, whereas New Jersey's trade with her neighbors was not. Second, only some of the west European core countries included peripheral regions; others did not include any. This implies that most of the peripheral products shipped into the west European core area were enumerated as international trade. The United States and Canada, on the other hand, included extensive and highly productive peripheral regions. Peripheral products shipped into the North American core area, therefore, originated largely within North America and were counted as international trade only if they were traded between the United States and Canada.

Jointly the core countries of Western Europe, North America, and Japan exported goods valued at $372 billion, or 70 percent of the world's total trade. Goods valued at $365 billion, somewhat less than 70 percent of the world's total trade, were imported by core countries. The core countries' trade with each other amounted to $254 billion, which was somewhat less than 70 percent of their total exports, but close to 70 percent of their total imports.

Compare this with the trade of the peripheral countries (including the developed, oil exporting, and poor peripheral countries distinguished in Table 1). In 1973 their exports were valued at $139 billion, and their imports at $142 billion. This accounted for little more than one-fourth of the world's international trade. The core countries took slightly over 70 percent of the peripheral countries' exports and supplied a nearly equal share of their imports. Trade among peripheral countries was relatively small.

To summarize: How many trade flows are recorded as international trade depends on the incidence of national boundaries. Given the current political divisions of the world, treating the centrally planned economies as a single unit, and taking 1973 as a representative year, we can make the following generalizations: approximately 70 percent of the world's international trade was conducted by core countries; roughly 70 percent of the core countries' trade took place among themselves; and roughly 70 percent of the peripheral countries' trade was conducted with core countries.

## Commodity Composition of International Trade

As we turn to the commodity composition of international trade, we shall limit our attention to the market economies. Statistics of their commodity exports and imports include trade with the centrally planned economies, but the centrally planned economies themselves will not be treated as a separate unit.

Our chief concern is to compare the trade of core and peripheral countries, and especially their trade in manufactured goods. Unfortunately, the Standard International Trade Classification (SITC), on which our tabulations necessarily are based, does not neatly separate manufactured from primary commodities. We shall follow the convention of designating SITC Sections 0, 1, 2, 3, and 4 as primary products, although a few commodities lumped with these Sections are properly manufactured goods.[4] Therefore, the trade in primary products is slightly overstated, and that in manufactured goods slightly understated.

We should note at the outset that there are several countries for which comparable commodity trade statistics for the year 1973 are lacking. These gaps are filled with estimates. When interpreting statistics based partly on estimates it is preferable to cite rough proportions rather than more precise

4. The notable instances are food preparations (lumped with Section 0), beverages and tobacco products (lumped with Section 1), and coke and petroleum products (lumped with Section 3). See *Standard International Trade Classification, Revised*, Statistical Papers Series M, No. 34 (New York: United Nations Statistical Office, 1961); and *Classification of Commodities by Industrial Origin — Relationship of the Standard International Trade Classification to the International Standard Industrial Classification*, Statistical Papers Series M, No. 43 (New York: United Nations Statistical Office, 1966).

31

## Table 2

### Exports and Imports of Core and Peripheral Countries, by Commodity Classes: 1973

#### (In Millions of Current U.S. Dollars)

| Commodity Classes | Exports, f.o.b. | | Imports, c.i.f.[a] | |
|---|---|---|---|---|
| | From Core Countries | From Peripheral Countries[b] | Of Core Countries | Of Peripheral Countries[b] |
| All Commodities .............. | 374,300 | 144,100 | 379,300 | 144,900 |
| Primary Products[c]............ | 82,000 | 97,500 | 145,900 | 43,100 |
| Manufactured Goods[d] ....... | 287,100 | 44,500 | 229,200 | 100,700 |
| Miscellaneous Goods[e] ....... | 5,200 | 2,100 | 4,200 | 1,100 |

[a]The imports of the following countries are valued f.o.b.: Australia, Bermuda, the British Virgin Islands, Canada, Papua and New Guinea, Paraguay, the Solomon Islands, South Africa, the United States, Venezuela, and Zambia.

[b]Based in part on estimates. For the following countries (ranked by their foreign trade turnover) commodity trade statistics were incomplete or not available at all: Taiwan, Peru, Zaire, Bangladesh, the Dominican Republic, Guatemala, Sri Lanka, Costa Rica, El Salvador, Mozambique, South Viet Nam, Panama, Uruguay, Gabon, Honduras, Bolivia, Surinam, Afghanistan, the Yemen Democratic Republic, Paraguay, Barbados, Mali, Mauritania, Somalia, Benin, Upper Volta, Chad, the Central African Empire, Belize, and the Cape Verde Islands.

[c]SITC Sections 0, 1, 2, 3, and 4.

[d]SITC Sections 5, 6, 7, and 8.

[e]SITC Section 9 and unclassified items.

Sources: *Yearbook of International Trade Statistics: 1975, Vol. I: Trade by Country* (New York: United Nations Statistical Office, 1976). Statistics of the trade between West and East Germany were supplied by the German American Chamber of Commerce in New York.

numerical values.

Despite the shortcomings of our data, it is safe to make the following observations: Considering the core countries as a group, their exports of manufactured goods were three and one-half times as great as their exports of primary products (Table 2). Considering the peripheral countries as a group, their exports of manufactured goods were less than one-half as great as their exports of primary products. The imports of the two groups of countries did not differ quite so drastically in commodity composition. Recalling that roughly 70 percent of the core countries' trade takes place among themselves, it should not be surprising to discover that the core countries' imports of manufactured goods exceeded their imports of primary products by a substantial margin. Nor should it be astonishing to find that the peripheral countries' imports of manufactured goods were well over twice as great as their imports of primary commodities. Peripheral countries, by definition, have a limited base of manufacturing industries; and this, of course, makes them dependent on imports of many manufactured items from core countries.

As we combine all the market economies, manufactured goods accounted for nearly two-thirds of their total exports and imports. Core countries were by far the chief exporters as well as the major importers of manufactured goods. Roughly six-sevenths of all the market economies' exports of manufactured goods originated in core countries, and approximately seven-tenths of all the market economies' imports of manufactured goods were received by core countries.

The conventional wisdom that core ("industrial") countries import mostly raw materials is patently wrong. Every core country except Italy and Japan imported more manufactured goods than primary products. By far most of the core countries' imports of manufactured goods came from other core countries. Only if one omitted the core countries' imports from each other could it be said that core countries imported mostly raw materials.

In 1973 the exports of peripheral countries consisted largely of primary products, but manufactured goods made up roughly three-tenths of the total (Table 2). As might be expected, most manufactured goods exported by peripheral countries derived from one or another type of peripheral industry. A few examples might be in order. The first type — industries whose dominant location factor is proximity to their major raw materials or source of power — accounted for the copper exports of Chile, Zambia, and Zaire; the tin exports of Malaysia and Bolivia; and the exports of paper and paperboard products from Finland. The second type — producers of finished goods other than capital goods for the manufacturing sector whose dominant location factor is proximity to their customers — did not generate much international trade, because the customers were usually domestic, not foreign. The third type of peripheral industry — factories whose dominant location factor is the availability of low-wage labor — accounted for exports of textiles and clothing from South Korea, Hong Kong, Macao, India, Israel, Bahrain, and Malta. Other examples are exports of electronic apparatus from South Korea, Hong Kong, and Singapore. The peripheral countries' exports of manufactured goods, however, were not limited to the products of peripheral industries, for two reasons: (1) A peripheral country may have had a few core industries, and some of these industries' products may have been exported. (2) A peripheral country may have exported products of core industries which previously had been imported from core countries. Not all that enters international trade is necessarily a product of the exporting country.[5]

Our distinction between core areas and periphery implies that core countries have a more diversified manufacturing sector than peripheral countries. Considering, furthermore,

---

5. The United Nations Statistical Office, in its endeavor to improve the international comparability of foreign trade statistics, has recommended that "merchandise in international trade shall include goods which add to or subtract from the stock of material resources in a country as a result of their movement into or out of the country." *International Trade Statistics — Concepts and Definitions*, Statistical Papers Series M, No. 52 (New York: United Nations Statistical Office, 1970), p. 3.

the great importance of manufactured goods in world trade, it is to be expected that the core countries' exports generally were more diversified, or less specialized, than those of peripheral countries.

This can be demonstrated with the help of Hirschman's index of specialization.[6] Applied to our problem, the index is

$$\sqrt{\sum_{i=1}^{n} P^2}$$

where $P$ designates the percentage which each commodity contributes to a country's total exports. The commodities in our case are the 182 SITC Groups which jointly comprise all merchandise traded. If only one commodity accounted for a country's total exports, the index would be 100. Index numbers below 100 can be interpreted as follows: The index number must necessarily be greater than the percentage which the highest ranking export commodity contributes to the total exports — but how much higher depends on the degree of specialization among the remaining export commodities.

The more detailed one's commodity classification, the smaller one's index is likely to be. Imagine a country which exports nothing but crude oil and petroleum products. If these were separate commodities (as in the SITC), the index would be smaller than 100. If, however, they were considered one commodity — on the grounds that they derived from just one natural resource — the index would be 100.

I have computed the index for the fourteen core countries and for those peripheral countries which ranked among the top twelve either in foreign trade turnover or in population, except that Taiwan (which ranked eleventh in trade turnover) and Bangladesh (which ranked fourth in population) had to be omitted for lack of comparable data on the commodity

6. Albert O. Hirschman, *National Power and the Structure of Foreign Trade* (Berkeley: University of California Press, 1945), pp. 98-99 and 157-162.

## Table 3
## Exports of Core and Peripheral Countries, Index
## of Commodity Specialization: 1973

| Core Countries | Index | Peripheral Countries | Index |
|---|---|---|---|
| Netherlands | 14.1 | Spain | 16.5 |
| Austria | 14.8 | Mexico | 18.3 |
| France | 15.4 | Turkey | 19.8 |
| United Kingdom | 16.3 | India | 20.3 |
| Belgium-Luxembourg | 16.6 | South Africa | 21.8 |
| United States | 16.9 | Thailand | 25.5 |
| Italy | 17.6 | Australia | 27.8 |
| West Germany[a] | 19.4 | Brazil | 28.0 |
| Switzerland | 20.2 | South Korea | 28.1 |
| Sweden | 20.5 | Singapore | 29.3 |
| Denmark | 21.2 | Finland | 30.7 |
| Japan | 21.9 | Hong Kong | 31.8 |
| Canada | 24.3 | Philippines | 32.3 |
| Norway | 25.1 | Pakistan | 34.8 |
| | | Egypt | 47.6 |
| | | Indonesia | 48.9 |
| | | Venezuela | 69.5 |
| | | Iran | 82.4 |
| | | Nigeria | 83.8 |
| | | Saudi Arabia | 92.4 |

[a] Excludes trade with East Germany.

Source: *Yearbook of International Trade Statistics: 1975*, Vol. I: *Trade by Country* (New York: United Nations Statistical Office, 1976).

composition of their exports. This has reduced the number of peripheral countries for which the index has been calculated to twenty.

On the basis of these data, it appears that the index of specialization in commodity exports ranged from 14.1 to 25.1 among the fourteen core countries, and from 16.5 to 92.4 among the twenty peripheral countries (Table 3). Of the peripheral countries, only five exhibited more diversification than the least diversified core country; but of the fourteen core countries, ten exhibited less diversification than the most diversified peripheral country.

Several of the peripheral countries with rather diversified exports had a more broadly based manufacturing sector than is typical of peripheral countries. This definitely applies to Spain, Mexico, Brazil, and India. It is not inconsistent with our theory. As noted earlier (Chapter 2), core areas do not originate overnight, and there are regions in a stage of transition from peripheral manufacturing center to fully developed core area. Northern Spain may become part of the west European core area, and new core areas may be developing in Mexico, Brazil, and India.

The conclusion which can be drawn from our data is that the exports of core countries tend to be quite diversified, and that this is attributable to their diversified manufacturing sector. Among peripheral countries there is a wide range in the index of export specialization, and this can be explained only with reference to the more or less unique situations of the particular countries involved.

## Four Types of Trade

According to our model of the world economy, four types of trade are possible, regardless of the incidence of national boundaries:

1. Trade within a core area, or intracore trade.
2. Trade between core areas, or intercore trade.

3. Trade between a core area and the periphery, or core-periphery trade.

4. Trade within the periphery, or intraperiphery trade.

The difference between these four types of trade is explained most readily in a historical context.

Prior to the Industrial Revolution, when there were no core areas, all trade was necessarily intraperiphery trade — as seen from our modern vantage point, of course. Transportation was by horse and buggy, on camel back, in wooden sailing vessels, or by some other primitive means. In any case, it was very risky and expensive by modern standards. Intraperiphery trade, therefore, consisted of an exchange of regional specialties of great value relative to their bulk. Examples of such regional specialties were silk, fine woolens and cotton cloth, Oriental rugs, honey, wine, dried or salted meat and fish, nonferrous metals, and precious stones. More bulky commodities such as raw wool, salt, and grains were traded over shorter distances.

With the Industrial Revolution the world's first core area emerged in Great Britain. When coke replaced charcoal in the reduction of iron ore, Great Britain became the first country to experience the evolution from a "vegetable civilization" to a "mineral civilization." Also, she became the first country to experience the shift from human and animal power to the mechanical power of the steam engine. Last but not least, her textile industry became the first to create a mass market for manufactured goods. Without a mass market the Industrial Revolution was inconceivable.

In the late eighteenth and early nineteenth centuries the core-periphery trade centered on Great Britain had a tremendous potential for expansion. This was the era of the classical economists, when Adam Smith found a receptive audience for his free trade doctrine, and when David Ricardo's exposition of the principle of comparative advantage became the basis of the theory of international economics.

It was the expansion of core-periphery trade which laid the foundation of the modern world economy. The commercial opportunities created by this trade gave rise to steamship, canal, and railroad transportation focused upon the growing core areas in Europe and North America. In the latter part of the nineteenth century a marked decline in transport costs created an intercontinental trade in bulk commodities such as grains and minerals. Nonetheless, core-periphery trade resembled the earlier intraperiphery trade. Both consisted primarily of an exchange of different commodities made by different industries using different resources and employing factors of production in different proportions. The factor proportions theorem (which was discussed briefly in Chapter 1) attempts to explain these types of trade.[7]

The beginnings of intracore trade date from the expansion of the British core area onto the European continent, and the beginnings of intercore trade from the growth of a second core area in North America. In intracore and intercore trade there is a sizable exchange of similar commodities, mostly manufactured goods, made by the same industry using similar or identical resources, technologies, and factors of production.[8] An obvious manifestation of intracore and intercore trade is the thriving trade in automobiles among core countries. The automobile trade among the west European core countries exemplifies intracore trade, and so does the automobile trade between the northeastern United States and the Ontario Peninsula of Canada. Intercore trade in automobiles is exemplified by exports from Western Europe and Japan to the North American core area.

An exchange of goods made by the same industry using virtually identical factors of production in the same propor-

---

7. The empirical examples cited in Ohlin's *Interregional and International Trade* relate mostly to core-periphery or intraperiphery trade.

8. By 1961 Andreas Predöhl and Harald Jürgensen had noted this kind of trade and coined the term *substitutiver Austausch* to designate it. See *Handwörterbuch der Sozialwissenschaften*, s.v. "Europäische Integration."

tions cannot be explained by the factor proportions theorem.[9] In the automobile trade the explanation seems to be product differentiation in response to consumer preferences, and economies of large scale production. In recent years, for instance, the French automobile industry specialized in the production of cars that gave good service and were economical in the use of gasoline, on which the French government had imposed exceptionally high taxes. In Italy there was a comparatively stronger demand for cars which were fast and elegant. Most Germans wanted cars which were solid and durable. Yet all of these cars were in demand beyond the countries where they were produced.[10]

In other cases recent inventions gave rise to an exchange of similar commodities. As noted earlier (Chapter 2), core areas are the chief centers of industrial inventions and innovations. Each core country, for example, traded its newest pharmaceutical products for other core countries' pharmaceutical products. Technological leads were a powerful incentive to trade.

Our argument, once more, is that an exchange of similar commodities, mostly manufactured goods, is characteristic of intracore and intercore trade, but not of core-periphery or intraperiphery trade. A comprehensive proof of this proposition, however, would require an enormous job of tabulating. The core countries' trade would have to be classified into flows representing either intracore, intercore, or core-

9. See Herbert G. Grubel and P. J. Lloyd, *Intra-Industry Trade — The Theory and Measurement of International Trade in Differentiated Products* (New York: John Wiley and Sons, 1975), especially pp. 133-139.

10. According to Staffan Burenstam Linder, the range of a country's exports of manufactured goods is determined by domestic demand. Only products demanded in the home market are manufactured, and only such products are potential export commodities. *An Essay on Trade and Transformation* (New York: John Wiley and Sons, 1961), pp. 87-107. This generalization, however, needs be qualified. It does not hold for the products of manufacturing industries whose dominant location factor is proximity to their major raw materials or power (the first type of peripheral manufacturing industry); nor does it hold for the products of manufacturing industries whose dominant location factor is the availability of low-wage labor (the third type of peripheral manufacturing industry).

periphery trade; and the peripheral countries' trade would have to be differentiated into either core-periphery or intraperiphery trade. Then, for each of these trade flows, commodity exports and imports would have to be tabulated at a level of disaggregation so that each commodity could be said to consist of similar items or items of the same type — such as automobiles, pharmaceutical products, etc. Such tabulations would be excessively tedious. Therefore, my endeavor is limited to calculating the same type of commodity exchange for the United Kingdom's trade with West Germany, Japan, and the eleven countries which constitute the Latin American Free Trade Association (LAFTA). The United Kingdom's trade with West Germany represents intracore, that with Japan intercore, and that with LAFTA core-periphery trade. As a surrogate for "commodities of the same type" I have chosen the 182 SITC Groups which jointly account for all merchandise trade.

How should the "same type of commodity exchange" be defined? Suppose a country exported automobiles valued at $400 million, and imported automobiles valued at $100 million. The trade turnover in automobiles would be $500 million. Of that, $300 million would be a net export. The remainder, $200 million, would be a same type of commodity exchange.

For any given SITC Group, the same type of commodity exchange $S_i$, may be defined as

$$S_i = X_i + M_i - | X_i - M_i |$$

where X stands for exports, M for imports, and the $i$ designate any SITC Group. The same type of commodity exchange is double the value of the exports or imports, whichever is smaller. Whatever is not a same type of commodity exchange is necessarily a net export or net import of that commodity.

For all SITC Groups or for SITC Sections, which comprise

Table 4

The United Kingdom's Same Type of Commodity Exchange
as a Percentage of Her Trade Turnover with
West Germany, Japan, and LAFTA: 1973

| SITC Sections[a] | West Germany | Japan | LAFTA[b] |
|---|---|---|---|
| All Commodities (182) .................. | 54.5 | 28.5 | 6.6 |
| Food and Live Animals (33) .................. | 51.4 | 3.8 | 1.4 |
| Beverages and Tobacco (4) .................. | 71.9 | 0.0 | 3.4 |
| Crude Materials Except Fuels (29) .................. | 35.9 | 8.6 | 2.1 |
| Mineral Fuels, Lubricants, and Related Materials (5) ......... | 74.8 | 69.6 | 3.4 |
| Animal and Vegetable Oils and Fats (4) ......... | 50.0 | 19.1 | 9.7 |
| Chemicals (16) .................. | 51.4 | 40.6 | 18.9 |
| Manufactured Goods Classified Chiefly by Material (50) ...... | 46.7 | 24.1 | 9.2 |
| Machinery and Transport Equipment (18) .................. | 58.2 | 30.2 | 9.8 |
| Miscellaneous Manufactured Goods (18) .................. | 61.1 | 39.9 | 14.3 |
| Goods not Classified by Kind (5) .................. | 11.8 | 0.0 | 0.0 |

[a] The figures in parentheses state the number of SITC Groups within each SITC Section.

[b] Includes Argentina, Bolivia, Brazil, Chile, Colombia, Ecuador, Mexico, Paraguay, Peru, Uruguay, and Venezuela.

Source: *Commodity Trade Statistics*, Statistical Papers Series D, Vol. 23, No. 34 (New York: United Nations Statistical Office, no date).

several SITC Groups, the same type of commodity exchange equals the sum of the $S_i$. As a percentage of the trade turnover the same type of commodity exchange equals

$$100 \sum_{i=1}^{n} S_i \left[ \sum_{i=1}^{n} (X_i + M_i) \right]^{-1}$$

These are the values reported above (Table 4).

One more technicality: In the United Kingdom's trade with West Germany, Japan, and LAFTA in 1973, there was a sizable import surplus on the part of the United Kingdom. Because of this, in the United Kingdom's total commodity trade with these countries the same type of commodity exchange could not possibly have reached 100 percent of the trade turnover. If for every export of an SITC Group there had been a matching import of that same SITC Group, the same type of commodity exchange for all SITC Groups as a percentage of the trade turnover would have been only 72.4 percent in the trade with West Germany, 74.6 percent in the trade with Japan, and 79.0 percent in the trade with LAFTA.

In view of this, it is remarkable that in the United Kingdom's trade with West Germany and Japan the same type of commodity exchange reached 54.5 and 28.5 percent of the turnover respectively, compared with only 6.6 percent in the trade with LAFTA (Table 4). This corresponds well with our contention that a same type of commodity exchange is more prevalent in intracore and intercore trade than in core-periphery trade.

## Summary

The modern world economy is focused upon core areas. Their characteristic — a complex of vertically integrated manufacturing industries — implies that they generate a large volume of trade within themselves, which we call intracore trade. Also, core areas carry on a sizable trade with each other, or intercore trade. The trade of peripheral regions is conducted mostly with core areas. This type of trade we call core-periphery trade. Trade within the periphery, or intraperiphery trade, is relatively small.

The modern transport network was laid out in response to the commercial opportunities created by the Industrial Revolution. It facilitates intracore, intercore, and core-periphery trade, but not intraperiphery trade.

The four types of trade differ in their commodity composition. Intracore and intercore trade consist largely of an exchange of similar types of goods. Much of the trade within and between core areas cannot be attributed to geographical differences in factor endowments, but occurs in response to recent inventions, technological leads, consumer preferences, and economies of large scale production. Core-periphery and intraperiphery trade, on the other hand, consist primarily of an exchange of different commodities made by different industries. Core-periphery trade is primarily an exchange of manufactured goods of core areas for primary products or for products of peripheral manufacturing industries. Intraperiphery trade is mostly an exchange of regional specialties, which may be primary products or manufactured goods.

From the viewpoint of the regional theory of world trade, national boundaries are superimposed arbitrarily upon core areas and peripheral regions. Given the present geographic pattern of national boundaries, core areas, and periphery, intercore trade is always counted as international trade. All other types of trade, however, are recorded in a most inconsistent manner. In the west European core area vastly more intracore trade is enumerated than in the North American core area. Core-periphery trade, likewise, is enumerated in a seemingly arbitrary manner. Of the core-periphery trade generated by the west European and Japanese core areas much is counted as international trade, but of the core-periphery trade generated by the North American core area much escapes enumeration. Intraperiphery trade, too, has a poor chance of being counted in North America — but a much better chance in Central America.

Most international trade statistics fail to reveal the type of trade which is involved. Trade between the United States and Japan, for instance, may be either intercore or core-periphery trade. Trade between the Netherlands and Italy may be either intracore or core-periphery trade. Obviously, the collection of international trade statistics takes place without regard for the regional economic structure of the world economy.

Yet when the geographic pattern of core areas and periphery and the divergent pattern of national territories are known, the flow of international trade is found to be consistent with the regional theory of world trade. Where international boundaries traverse a core area, a great volume of trade is necessarily enumerated. This explains why in 1973 the eleven core countries of Western Europe traded goods valued at $150 billion with each other, whereas the peripheral market economies, of which there were 143, traded goods valued at only $34 billion with each other.

# 4

# A LOOK TO THE FUTURE

THE WORLD ECONOMY is changing. New opportunities to trade provide new incentives for economic growth. Consider the case of Latin America. A century ago Latin America's trade was oriented primarily toward Europe. In the latter part of the nineteenth century the growth of the North American core area caused a shift in Latin America's trade patterns and provided a new impetus to Latin America's economic development. More recently, the commercial expansion of the Japanese core area brought about another shift in Latin America's trade patterns and provided an added stimulus to Latin America's economic growth. Nonetheless, thus far Latin America has remained an underdeveloped region — or a series of more or less underdeveloped regions.

## Imbalance of Core Areas and Periphery

Approximately 88 percent of the world's people live in peripheral regions, and 78 percent live in peripheral countries (Figure 2). Considering only market economies, the proportions are similar: 86 percent live in peripheral regions, and 77 percent live in peripheral countries. At the same time, it is evident that in many peripheral areas human resources are underdeveloped. Huge numbers of potentially more productive workers are undernourished, diseased, unskilled, and underemployed.

Peripheral economies are not necessarily unproductive. Some peripheral areas — near or far from existing core areas, within or outside core countries — are fully integrated with the world economy. In such peripheral areas the development of human resources and per capita incomes are in fact equivalent to those in core areas. Most of the periphery, however, is not fully integrated with the world economy; there human resources are underdeveloped, and per capita incomes are low. Nations which include both types of areas — areas which are integrated with the world economy as well as areas which are not — are said to have "dual economies."

For the periphery, integration with the world economy involves the development of core-periphery trade. Core areas and periphery are interdependent. Their relationship, however, is not one among equals. Core areas are the growth poles, or the recession poles, of the world economy. This was evident during the expansive phase of the European and North American core areas before World War I as well as during the Great Depression. It is equally true today. Core areas can promote the economic growth of the periphery through trade and investments, because core areas command the necessary markets, capital, technology, and organization. But peripheral areas cannot promote the economic growth of core areas, because peripheral areas lack most or all of these prerequisites. Several OPEC members command substantial capital resources, but cannot furnish the large markets, modern technology, and effective organization necessary to promote the economic growth of core areas.

The underdevelopment of human resources, which is so evident in most peripheral regions, is commonly attributed to preindustrial institutions represented by vested interests which claim important privileges for themselves. One may acccpt this explanation, and yet one may wonder why exclusive groups and outmoded institutions have been able to persist in most peripheral regions. After all, institutions and

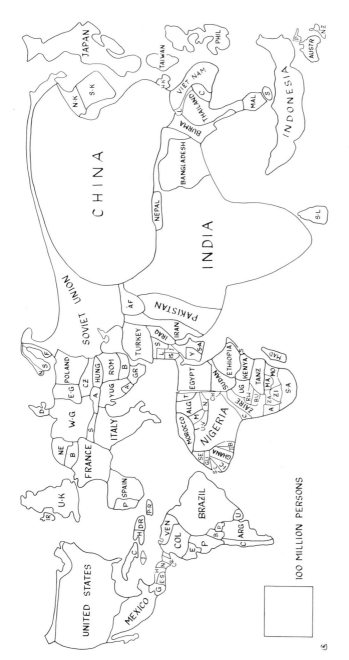

**Figure 2 — Countries proportional to their population in 1973. Compare with Figure 1.**

49

vested interests are not immutable. As societies evolve, the vested interests of an earlier age are replaced by those of a later age, and new privileges are seized by other groups. It is naive to believe that privileges can be abolished.[1] Speaking of modern democracies, James Russell Lowell has noted that "... what men prize most is a privilege, even if it be that of the chief mourner at a funeral."[2] Yet it is true as well as significant that wherever human resources are more fully developed, privileges are shared more widely, and only so-called "minorities" (including women) are said to be "under-privileged."

What we need, then, is an explanation of the underdevelopment of human resources as well as of the persistence of outmoded institutions and exclusive interests in most peripheral regions. That explanation, I suggest, is the failure of the existing core areas to generate adequate incentives for all of the periphery's economic and social advancement. As Ragnar Nurkse has suggested two decades ago, the "engine of growth," which prior to World War I had transmitted the economic advancement of the European and North American core areas to the periphery, has ceased to function efficiently.[3] Prior to World War I the engine was fueled by an increasing demand in the core areas for the products of peripheral regions. At that time the populations of the European and North American core areas were increasing rapidly, and the per capita consumption of material goods was increasing, too. Since then, population growth in these large core areas has been modest, whereas the population and potential labor force of most peripheral areas have increased substantially (Figure 3.)

1. There are those who insist that communism does not serve vested interests and does not tolerate privilege. But empirical evidence belies their contentions.

2. James Russell Lowell, "Democracy — Inaugural Address on Assuming the Presidency of the Birmingham and Midland Institute, Birmingham, England, 6 October 1884," in The Complete Writings of James Russell Lowell, Vol. 7: Literary and Political Adresses (New York: AMS Press, 1966), pp. 3-37, quote from p. 28.

3. Ragnar Nurkse, Patterns of Trade and Development, Wicksell Lectures 1959 (Stockholm: Almqvist and Wiksell, 1959).

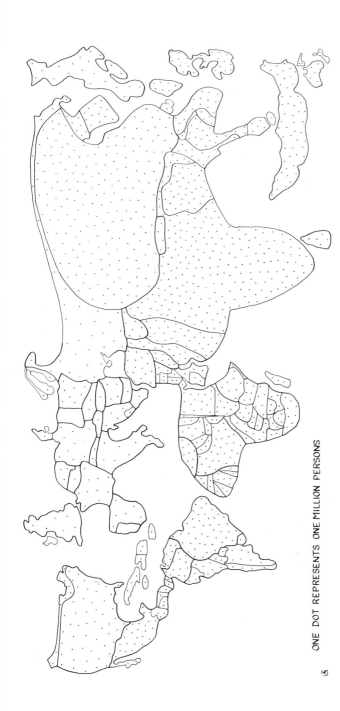

ONE DOT REPRESENTS ONE MILLION PERSONS

**Figure 3** — Population increase from 1953 to 1973. The number of dots is proportional to the absolute increase, their density to the rate of increase.

51

After the Great Depression the economic growth of the older, established core areas has been mostly in the service sector — conspicuously in social and medical services and in vocational and higher education. The service sector is labor and capital intensive and does not generate much demand for the products of the periphery.

Food production in the west European, North American, and Japanese core areas has increased with the application of chemical fertilizers and other technological innovations. At the same time, the agricultural sectors of the core countries were protected from competing with more efficient producers of sugar, grains, and animal products in peripheral countries. The core countries' textile industries, faced with competition from peripheral countries in Asia, the Caribbean, and Latin America, were protected by import quotas. Electronic components made in peripheral countries, commonly by subsidiaries of companies headquarterd in core countries, have been a more successful export commodity thus far. This export opportunity, however, is threatened also by an ever more insistent demand in core countries to curtail imports from low-wage peripheral countries. In the United States companies which maintain production facilities in foreign countries are accused by labor leaders of "exporting American jobs."

Several export commodities of the periphery are being replaced with goods produced within core areas. Synthetic dyes have replaced indigo, and nylon has replaced silk for most purposes. Synthetic rubber competes with natural rubber; synthetic fibers compete with cotton, wool, jute, and hemp; and fiberglass and plastics compete with tropical hardwoods and leather. Other materials imported from the periphery, such as copper and tin, are used more sparingly and may be recycled. The outstanding exception among peripheral export commodities is oil, for which the west European, North American, and Japanese core areas have provided rapidly expanding markets until recently, and they probably will be sizable markets for some time to come. Most of the periphery, however, depends for its export earnings on commodities for which the market is limited or which face stringent import restrictions in core countries.

The expansive forces of the existing core areas have been spent and, for the reasons just cited, are not likely to be rejuvenated. The prevailing trend in recent decades has been a decline in core-periphery trade relative to intracore and intercore trade. Peripheral countries, except those exporting oil, have furnished an ever smaller share of the imports of the west European core countries, the United States, Canada, and Japan (Table 5). The poorest of the peripheral countries fared

Table 5

Combined Imports of the West European Core Countries,
the United States, Canada, and Japan,
by Origin: 1953, 1963, and 1973
(In Percent of Total Imports)

| Origin of Imports | 1953 | 1963 | 1973 |
|---|---|---|---|
| All Countries ............................. | 100.00 | 100.00 | 100.00 |
| West European Core Countries, United States, Canada, and Japan ............... | 55.6 | 66.3 | 69.6 |
| Centrally Planned Economies ............ | 3.2 | 3.6 | 3.6 |
| Developed Peripheral Countries .......... | 9.8 | 6.9 | 6.4 |
| Oil Exporting Countries .................. | 9.0 | 7.7 | 8.6 |
| Poor Peripheral Countries ................ | 22.4 | 15.5 | 11.8 |

Note: The definitions are the same as for Table 1. To assure chronological comparability, Cuba has been included with the centrally planned economies throughout. If Cuba had been included with the poor peripheral countries in 1953, their share of the imports of the west European core countries, the United States, Canada, and Japan would have been 23.8 percent, and that of the centrally planned economies would have been 1.8 percent.

Sources: *Direction of Trade: Annual 1970-74* and *1960-64* (Washington, D.C.: International Monetary Fund and International Bank for Reconstruction and Development, no dates); *Direction of International Trade,* Statistical Papers Series T, Vol. 8, No. 7 (New York: United Nations Statistical Office, International Monetary Fund, and International Bank for Reconstruction and Development, 1957); and trade data between West and East Germany supplied by the German American Chamber of Commerce in New York.

the worst; in 1953 they supplied 22.4 percent of the core countries' imports, in 1963 only 15.5 percent, and by 1973 merely 11.8 percent.

At the same time, the potential labor resources of most peripheral countries have expanded chiefly as a result of declining death rates. The development of those potential labor resources presupposes appropriate incentives. Thus far, the opportunities for productive employment have been grossly inadequate, especially in the poorest peripheral countries. This is the basic reason for their low per capita income. To say that the poor, underdeveloped countries must transform their economies is to say merely the obvious.[4] Nor is it profound to say that such a transformation must involve industrialization. An economy which is not industrialized (by any conventional interpretation of that term) cannot be efficient by modern standards.

Conventional wisdom holds that the engine of growth belongs to the past.[5] This assertion is based on a static view of the world economy which I do not accept. True, the existing core areas do not generate adequate incentives for all of the periphery's economic and social advancement; the engine lacks the necessary fuel — an increasing demand for the raw materials and manufactured products of the periphery. The world economy, however, is subject to change. As new core

---

4. Staffan Burenstam Linder has proposed that there are underdeveloped countries — so-called "u-countries" — which lack the ability to reallocate resources. *An Essay on Trade and Transformation*, pp. 11-48. In my view the notion that there are countries whose resources are totally immobile and whose economies are unable to respond to external commercial stimuli seems a theorist's nightmare rather than a realistic proposition.

5. Charles P. Kindleberger, for example, has written: "It will be of particular importance to consider Ragnar Nurkse's view that external stimuli to growth and industrialization were inherent in the pattern of the nineteenth century, but are no longer relevant in the twentieth, except perhaps in oil." After examining this thesis, Kindleberger has given it qualified support. *Foreign Trade and the National Economy* (New Haven: Yale University Press, 1962), pp. 195-196 and 205. More recently an equally pessimistic view has been presented by Carlos F. Diaz-Alejandro, "Trade Policies and Economic Development," in *International Trade and Finance — Frontiers for Research*, ed. Peter B. Kenen (Cambridge, England: Cambridge University Press, 1975), pp. 93-150, especially pp. 103-108.

areas come into existence, the engine will be set in motion again. After all, there is a rational basis for core-periphery trade and for the flow of technology and long-term investments from core areas to the periphery.

The relevant question, therefore, is: which peripheral regions present opportunities for core area growth? Only some regions have the potential to develop and sustain a complex of vertically integrated manufacturing industries. As the existing core areas have in the past, so future core areas will hereafter constitute growth poles for the remaining peripheral regions.

## Opportunities for Core Area Growth

The development of new core areas is likely set in motion by existing peripheral manufacturing industries through their backward and forward linkages.[6] A few examples may help to substantiate this point.

The first type of peripheral industry comprises factories whose dominant location factor is proximity to their raw materials or source of power. Among them are the sugar mills of Puerto Rico, which by their forward linkages have given rise to rum distilleries and paper mills. The former use molasses, the latter bagasse — both by-products of sugar cane processing. The sugar mills represent a peripheral industry; but the rum distilleries and paper mills are core industries, because their dominant location factor is proximity to other manufacturing plants, namely the sugar mills.

---

6. This notion is quite compatible with the models of industrial growth espoused by many development economists. See, for instance, Albert O. Hirschman, *The Strategy of Economic Development* (New Haven: Yale University Press, 1958), especially pp. 98-119; and George B. Baldwin, "Industrialization: A Standard Pattern," *Finance and Development*, Vol. 3 (December 1966), pp. 274-282. It differs from the theory proposed by Walther G. Hoffmann, which postulates that the growth of a country's manufacturing sector goes through stages marked by an increase of capital goods industries relative to consumer goods industries. See *The Growth of Industrial Economies*, trans. W. O. Henderson and W. H. Chaloner (Manchester: Manchester University Press, 1958).

Other examples are the oil refineries and ammonia or urea plants in Texas, Venezuela, Kuwait, and elsewhere, whose dominant location factor is proximity to crude oil and natural gas. By their forward linkages they have given rise to petrochemical and fertilizer plants, which are core industries.

Inasmuch as raw material-oriented factories require inputs of manufactured supplies, they may attract core industries by their backward linkages. Fruit, vegetable, and fish processing plants, for instance, may attract producers of suitable containers. Or a power-oriented aluminum refinery, as on the lower Mississippi River near New Orleans, may attract an alumina plant. The alumina plant is a core industry, because its dominant location factor is proximity to the aluminum refinery — another manufacturing plant.

The second type of peripheral industry comprises producers of finished goods for the primary or service sectors (including households) whose dominant location factor is proximity to their customers. Market-oriented automobile assembly plants are an example. By their backward linkages such industries may give rise to ancillary industries. This process has stimulated the growth of the motor vehicle industries of Mexico, Brazil, India, and Australia. These industries had been initiated by assembly plants which at first depended on imported components, but later relied increasingly on parts furnished by domestic suppliers. In Brazil there are now over 1,500 firms manufacturing parts and components for passenger cars and trucks.[7]

The third type of peripheral industry includes factories whose dominant location factor is the availability of low-wage labor. Hong Kong's textile, apparel, and electronics industries belong to this type. Through subcontracting arrangements they have stimulated the growth of related industries. A recent study reports:

---

7. Joel Bergsman, *Brazil — Industrialization and Trade Policies* (New York: Oxford University Press for the Organization for Economic Co-operation and Development, 1970), p. 122.

Both the rapid growth and diversification of the Hong Kong economy and the characteristics of many of its consumer-goods industries and their markets are conducive to a substantial amount of subcontracting among manufacturing firms. Especially in the clothing industries, the larger factories often seek or receive more orders than they can fill with their existing capacity in the time required. However, the volatility of demand for particular types of garments and styles, the difficulty of recruiting and training additional labor, the greater profitability of other possible investments, the problems of directly managing a bigger or more diverse production process or, in the case of textiles, the limitations of the export quotas assigned to them under the "voluntary restraint" agreements, dissuade them from expanding their own facilities. Or, certain sewing and finishing operations can more profitably be delegated to subcontractors than carried on in the firm's own factory because the former have smaller overhead expenses or are willing to realize smaller profit margins. Such conditions fostering subcontracting are also prevalent in other Hong Kong industries.[8]

It is not to be expected, of course, that in any conceivable location a few core industries necessarily will initiate the growth of a core area sufficiently large and diversified to have a significant impact upon the world economy. Core areas which focus the trade of sizable peripheral regions upon themselves and constitute growth poles for such regions can arise only in large, densely settled regions. Only such regions are capable of furnishing a large industrial labor force, a comprehensive array of business, transportation, and research services, and a large market for their own products

8. Theodore Geiger and Frances M. Geiger, *Tales of Two City-States: The Development Progress of Hong Kong and Singapore*, Studies in Development Progress No. 3 (Washington, D.C.: National Planning Association, 1973), p. 76.

and for those of peripheral regions. From this point of view, the potential for core area development seems best in the Bengal-Bihar-Orissa region of India, in northeastern China, in Mexico, in southeastern Brazil, or possibly in a larger region extending from there to the Rio de la Plata estuary.[9]

Referring to the potential for core area growth in India and China, Hans-Jürgen Harborth has written:

> To point out the factor of population size and density as an essential condition for the formation of industrial centres may seem unusual — especially as it is the densely populated developing countries, continually threatened with famine, that are the strongest contrast conceivable to the advanced industrial centres of the world economy. But this does not in any way alter the fact that concentrations of populations in China or India, for example, are at the same time huge concentrations of potential factors of production and of demand which definitely favour the development of an industrial structure in breadth.[10]

Indeed, the fact that Japan has developed a significant core area thus far, whereas Australia has not, would be difficult to explain without recourse to Australia's relatively smaller population and limited domestic market.

## Summary

Core areas are the growth poles, or recession poles, of the

9. The possibility of a core area including the major population and industrial concentrations of Brazil, Uruguay, and Argentina has been suggested in Hans-Jürgen Harborth, *Neue Industriezentren an der weltwirtschaftlichen Peripherie* (Hamburg: Hoffmann und Campe for the Deutsche Übersee-Institut, 1967), p. 71.

10. Hans-Jürgen Harborth, "On the Role of Developing Countires in a Multicentric World Economy," *Economics — A Biannual Collection of Recent German Contributions to the Field of Economic Science*, Vol. 5 (1972), pp. 68-83, quote from pp. 75-76.

world economy. They can promote the economic development of the periphery through trade and investments, because they command the necessary markets, capital, technology, and organization. But the periphery cannot promote the economic growth of core areas, because it lacks most or all of these prerequisites.

Peripheral economies may be highly productive and attain a high income for the vast majority of their inhabitants. Yet most peripheral areas have remained underdeveloped. The crushing poverty which prevails in most of the periphery today attests to the failure of the existing core areas to generate adequate incentives for all of the periphery's productive development. There exists an imbalance in the regional structure of the world economy which can be overcome only by the growth of new core areas.

Core areas large enough to have a significant impact upon the world economy — to constitute growth poles for sizable peripheral regions — can arise only in large, densely settled areas capable of furnishing an adequate industrial labor force, a comprehensive infrastructure of financial, transportation, and technological services, and a broadly based market for their own products and for those of the periphery.

Some form of regional differentiation between core areas and periphery will persist, although the specific geographic patterns of core areas and periphery will change. As new core areas evolve, they will focus the trade of the remaining peripheral areas upon themselves and function as growth poles. The Japanese core area has been the latest to develop thus far. Council of despair notwithstanding, I suggest that it will not be the last one before doomsday. Without the growth of new core areas there is no realistic hope for a world economy in which the opportunities for economic advancement are shared more equitably.

# 5

# LIMITATIONS OF THE THEORY

IN THREE RESPECTS the regional theory of world trade departs from conventional habits of thinking:

(1) Its basic concern is not with the trade of nations, but with the trade of core areas and the periphery. This, however, does not make the theory inapplicable to an explanation of international trade· it only means that such an explanation must be based on the underlying geographic pattern of core areas and periphery.

(2) The regional theory is incompatible with the widely held notion that industries classified by their products exhibit the same location characteristics. Steel mills, pharmaceutical plants, electronics factories, and many others, depending on their dominant location factors, may be either core or peripheral industries. In some cases specific investigations are necessary to determine the dominant location factor of a particular plant. Furthermore, the regional theory, like the product life cycle theory, assumes that industries producing specific goods may change their location characteristics through time.

(3) The regional theory, following Weber's theory of industrial location, restricts the term *raw* material-oriented manufacturing industry to one whose dominant location factor is proximity to one or several primary producers who

61

supply that industry's major inputs. But transport economies may draw an industry also to suppliers of inputs of intermediate manufactured goods. Thus, many subsequent location theorists have stretched the term "raw material-oriented" industry to cover one whose dominant location factor is proximity to its suppliers of intermediate goods. This corruption of terminology could have been avoided. Edgar M. Hoover, for instance, has used the terms "material-" or "input-oriented" industries to designate those drawn to the sources of their material inputs which might be either primary products or intermediate manufactured goods.[1] Terminology is important in this case. The regional theory rests on the distinction between core areas and periphery. That distinction is based on a classification of manufacturing industries by their location characteristics. That classification, in turn, makes sense only if it is recognized that raw materials are primary products, that intermediate goods are manufactured goods, that intermediate goods cannot be raw materials, and that manufactured goods cannot be primary products.

The fatal blow to the regional theory would be an obliteration of the difference between core areas and periphery. That is most improbable because of the tendency of core industries to agglomerate in large, densely settled regions. A rather likely development, however, is that core industries will become increasingly dispersed. Economies in transportation make such a dispersal feasible. The diseconomies of congestion as well as public restrictions on air and water pollution in older industrial centers reinforce a dispersal of core industries in peacetime, as strategic considerations have reinforced it in wartime. Most likely, core areas will become less compact and their delineation more difficult and less certain.

The regional theory recognizes several core areas, but only

1. Edgar M. Hoover, *The Location of Economic Activity*, paperback ed. (New York: McGraw-Hill, 1963), pp. 31-35; and idem, *An Introduction to Regional Economics* (New York: Alfred A. Knopf, 1971), p. 23.

one vast, undifferentiated periphery. The several core areas have developed at different times and have played different roles in the evolution of the world economy. Presently each core area comprises a geographically separate focus of commerce. In the context of the regional theory this appears to be merely an accident of geography and history. There are some differences among the present core areas in their industrial structure and in the trade which they generate, but those differences cannot be explained by the regional theory in its present state. In terms of the regional theory there seems to be no significant difference between intercore and intracore trade.[2]

It might well be argued that peripheral regions, however delineated, exhibit greater differences in their industrial structure than the several core areas. Yet the regional theory fails to differentiate among peripheral regions and thus fails to distinguish between intraperiphery and interperiphery trade. Such a distinction would make sense only if it could be shown that intraperiphery and interperiphery trade differed in some respect that can be explained by the regional theory.[3] Can anyone make such a distinction?

2. Predöhl has argued that intracore trade takes precedence over intercore trade; that during the post-World War II era the economic integration of the west European core area necessarily had to precede a world-wide economic integration; and that the recovery of the West German economy was attributable to its reintegration with the west European core area. See his *Aussenwirtschaft*, pp. 142 and 226-229. I am skeptical about this thesis. An examination of the relevant facts suggests that after 1958 West Germany's economic growth might have been furthered more by intercore trade (notably with the United States) than by intracore trade (notably with the other charter members of the European Coal and Steel Community and the European Economic Community). See my paper "West Germany's Economic Growth," *Annals of the Association of American Geographers*, Vol. 63 (September 1973), pp. 353-365.

3. Predöhl has introduced the concept of the *Wirtschaftsraum*, which includes just one core area and the periphery oriented toward that core area. But at the same time he has insisted that a *Wirtschaftsraum* is not a clearly delineated area (presumably because many peripheral regions carry on a substantial trade with several core areas). See his *Aussenwirtschaft*, pp. 72-73 and passim. An *indefinite* differentiation of the periphery into *Wirtschaftsräume*, of course, does not permit a *definite* distinction between intraperiphery and interperiphery trade.

Future studies may call for a revision of the theory or for amendments. At this stage a study of the effects of LAFTA seems especially worthwhile. LAFTA was chartered in 1960. Its objective was to stimulate over a very large area the growth of manufacturing industries whose products would displace imports from the established core areas in Western Europe, North America, and Japan. The manufacturing of many such products requires a complex of vertically integrated industries, and the removal of trade restrictions among the members of LAFTA was intended to facilitate the growth of such a complex. But Latin America's envisioned core area, unlike those already in existence elsewhere, was to consist of several fragmented parts located as far apart as Mexico City and Buenos Aires. Although no proponent of LAFTA has stated the organization's objectives in such stark terms, this was in fact its intention.[4]

Was such a project feasible? After all, a dispersal of core industries presupposes an efficient system of transportation. The distance from Mexico City to Buenos Aires is roughly five times that from New York to St. Louis, or four times that from Marseille to Stockholm. The construction and maintenance of rail and paved highway transportation over such an enormous distance, with connections to all major industrial centers along the way, seems prohibitively expensive. Maritime transport, although relatively cheaper, is slow and can reach only deep water locations. In recent years most of the commerce among Latin American countries was carried by sea; and yet, despite the prominence of maritime transportation, most Latin American port facilities were outmoded and

---

4. Galo Plaza, Chairman of the Working Group on the Latin American Regional Market of the United Nations Economic Commission for Latin America, has argued that an equal advancement of all Latin American countries required an equal level of industrial development, that the industrial structure of the regional market would have to be negotiated among the member governments, and that countries which thus far had not produced capital goods would require preferential treatment to foster capital goods industries on their territory. "For a Regional Market in Latin America," *Foreign Affairs*, Vol. 37 (July 1959), pp. 607-616.

inefficient.[5] Can it be said that despite these handicaps the core industries of LAFTA collectively have combined to form a vertically integrated complex? Or have they remained a series of smaller, specialized complexes which might have developed just the same without LAFTA?

Similar questions might be raised about the Latin American Economic System, known by its Spanish acronym SELA, which was initiated in 1975 and comprises all countries of the western hemisphere except Canada, the United States, and the Bahamas. Also, such questions might be asked about the Andean Group, which was created in 1969 and includes Peru, Bolivia, Ecuador, Colombia, and Venezuela (Chile withdrew in 1976). Collectively the Andean Group may comprise a potential market and labor force barely large enough for core area development. But is it feasible to divide a complex of vertically integrated industries into segments and scatter them over such a vast, largely mountainous and sparsely inhabited territory?[6] Can transport costs among widely separated industrial districts be kept so low that each district's final product can be sold in all the districts at prices which consumers can afford? What is involved, of course, are shipments of intermediate as well as finished goods.

Conventional wisdom attributes LAFTA's failures to conflicting national interests. When each nation insists on obtaining an "equitable" share of core industries, political agreement over the distribution of core industries is difficult

---

5. Enrique Angulo H., "Transportation and Intra-Latin American Trade, " in *Latin American Economic Integration — Experiences and Prospects*, ed. Miguel S. Wionczek (New York: Frederick A. Praeger, 1966), pp. 177-195. The inadequacy of rail and motor road transportation in Latin America are summarized in Nino Maritano, *A Latin American Economic Community — History, Policies, and Problems* (Notre Dame: University of Notre Dame Press, 1970), pp. 128-129. More recently unpaved highways have penetrated far into the Amazon Basin. But the intent of this project has been to make previously undeveloped areas accessible to settlers — not to provide linkages among existing or prospective manufacturing centers.

6. For the inadequacies of the transportation and communication networks within and among the Andean Group countries see David Morawetz, *The Andean Group: A Case Study in Economic Integration among Developing Countries* (Cambridge, Massachusetts: MIT Press, 1974), pp. 9-24.

to achieve. Although there is much truth in this explanation of LAFTA's failures, I believe that it avoids the basic economic issue. For the sake of argument, suppose that the whole of Latin America were placed under a centralized authoritarian government which decreed an "equitable" distribution of core industries. The political bickering would thereby be eliminated. Would that make it feasible to distribute core industries over the entire Latin American region? Surely not. It seems rather obvious that the cost of such a project would be staggering — so high as to frustrate any hopes for a general improvement in the standard of living in the foreseeable future. Applying LAFTA's precept to the United States, one might propose a development project based on an "equitable" distribution of core industries by Congressional districts!

This is not a council against Latin American economic integration. In my view, the relevant issue involves a choice between two options. Both options envisage the growth of manufacturing industries and the expansion of transport facilities among the Latin American countries.

One option is that contemplated by LAFTA. It necessitates the building and maintenance of a vast and intricate transport network which serves a hypothetical core area fragmented into several widely separated parts. Many core industries would be relegated to uneconomic locations and therefore require tariff protection or subsidies. This option is incompatible with a freely competitive economy within the Latin American region as a whole. The designation "Latin American Free Trade Association" is a misnomer.

The other option involves the building and maintenance of a less elaborate transport network focused on one or two compact, populous regions where core industries become concentrated. If this option were accepted, the prospective core areas would function as growth poles for the remaining peripheral areas which would develop, inter alia, peripheral manufacturing industries.[7] This is compatible with a freely

7. The second option might also be described as a concentration of core industries along "growth corridors" connecting existing metropolitan centers,

competitive economy within the Latin American region, but may necessitate infant industry tariffs for the region as a whole to protect its budding core industries from more seasoned competitors in Western Europe, North America, and Japan.

The obvious discrepancy between Latin America's economic aspirations and accomplishments thus far suggests the inadequacy of our knowledge regarding the opportunities and limitations of core area growth. Such knowledge is a necessary prerequisite for the proposal of realistic policies on which depend the future of a large portion of mankind.

---

and the development of "natural resource complexes" focused on the growth corridors. Stated in these terms, it is compatible, if not identical, with a development option discussed in Poul Ove Pedersen and Walter Stöhr, "Economic Integration and the Spatial Development of South America," *The American Behavioral Scientist*, Vol. 12 (May-June 1969), pp. 2-12.

# BIBLIOGRAPHY

THE REGIONAL THEORY OF WORLD TRADE draws upon concepts developed by international economists, location theorists, economic geographers, and development economists. The pertinent literature is grouped here under the following headings:

*General Studies of World Trade*
*Factor Proportions Theorem*
*Regional Models of World Trade*
*Industrial Location, Linkage, and Growth*
*The Impact of Technology on Industrial Location and the*
  *Patterns of Trade*
*The Imbalance of Core Areas and Periphery*
*Territorial Units: Nations, Customs Unions, and the*
  *Multinational Enterprise*
*Trade Statistics*

Related works are listed next to each other rather than in alphabetical or strictly chronological order. The annotations are intended to demonstrate the significance of the works cited to empirical studies of trade patterns in general and to the regional theory of world trade in particular.

## General Studies of World Trade

Condliffe, John B. *The Commerce of Nations.* New York: W. W. Norton, 1950.

  Relates the evolution of trade to the changing ideological, social, and political framework which was partly created by trade and within which trade had to function. The broad historical perspective makes this an exceptionally valuable book.

Kindleberger, Charles P. *Foreign Trade and the National Economy.* New Haven: Yale University Press, 1962.

  A comparative study of the significance of foreign trade to national economies — market and centrally planned economies, developed and underdeveloped countries. The discussion focuses on two main questions: (1) what determines the commodity composition and volume of countries' exports and imports, and (2) how is a country's foreign trade related to its domestic economy? The discourse is lively and supported with much empirical evidence; abstruse theoretical issues are brushed aside. The book provides an excellent summary of innovative approaches to the study of international trade up to 1962.

## Factor Proportions Theorem

Ohlin, Bertil. *Interregional and International Trade.* Rev. ed. Cambridge, Massachusetts: Harvard University Press, 1967.

The basic text on the factor proportions, or Heckscher-Ohlin, theorem. Published thirty-four years after the first edition, it includes a retrospective appendix by the author.

Samuelson, Paul A. "International Trade and the Equalisation of Factor Prices." *Economic Journal,* Vol. 58 (June 1948), pp. 163-184.

——. "International Factor Price Equalisation Once Again." *Economic Journal,* Vol. 59 (June 1949), pp. 181-197.

If the factor proportions theorem is to be valid, the techniques of producing a given good must be the same in all regions. The last proposition, in turn, is based on the factor price equalisation theorem, which asserts that trade tends to equalize the prices of factors of production. These two papers prove the theoretical validity of the factor price equalization theorem, but the proof is contingent upon several unrealistic premises, such as constant returns to scale in the production of goods and the absence of transport costs among regions.

Leontief, Wassily. "Domestic Production and Foreign Trade; the American Capital Position Re-Examined." *Proceedings of the American Philosophical Society,* Vol. 97 (September 1953), pp. 332-349. Reprinted in Leontief, Wassily. *Input-Output Economics,* pp. 68-99. New York: Oxford University Press, 1966.

——. "Factor Proportions and the Structure of American Trade: Further Theoretical and Empirical Analysis." *Review of Economics and Statistics,* Vol. 38 (November 1956), pp. 386-407. Reprinted in Leontief, Wassily. *Input-*

*Output Economics,* pp. 100-133. New York: Oxford University Press, 1966.

These two papers, based on an input-output analysis of the United States economy in 1947, reveal that the capital/labor ratio was lower in industries producing commodities for export than in industries producing commodities in competition with imports. If, as postulated by the factor proportions theorem, the techniques of producing a given commodity were the same in the United States and abroad, Leontief's finding would indicate that the United States was poorly endowed with capital and richly endowed with labor relative to the rest of the world, and therefore exported labor intensive goods and imported capital intensive goods. Leontief attributed his finding to the greater productivity of American workers relative to foreign workers and noted that professional, technical, and skilled labor comprised a larger share of the labor force in industries producing commodities for export than in industries producing commodities in competition with imports.

Ford, J. L. "The Ohlin-Heckscher Theory of the Basis of Commodity Trade." *Economic Journal,* Vol. 73 (September 1963), pp. 458-476.

This paper focuses on Ohlin's proposition that the techniques of producing a given commodity are identical in all regions. If this were realistic, Leontief's finding that the United States imported goods which, if produced domestically, would have been produced by techniques more capital intensive than the techniques used by United States export industries, necessarily would lead to the conclusion that the United States was, relative to the rest of the world, richly endowed with labor and poorly endowed with capital. If, however, the proposition of identical production techniques were unrealistic, Leontief's finding would not substantiate such a conclusion. According to Ford it is entirely conceivable that the United States imported goods which were produced by capital intensive techniques domestically, but by labor intensive techniques abroad. The paper goes on to demonstrate that without the proposition of identical production techniques in all regions the factor proportions theorem is untenable.

Minhas, Bagicha Singh. *An International Comparison of Factor Costs and Factor Use.* Amsterdam: North-Holland Publishing Company, 1963.

Empirical evidence demonstrates that manufacturing industries have considerable flexibility in substituting one factor of production for another. The elasticities of substitution, however, are lowest in the most profitable, competitive industries.

Viner, Jacob. "Relative Abundance of the Factors and International Trade." *Indian Economic Journal,* Vol. 9

(January 1962), pp. 274-288.

The most comprehensive and incisive criticism of the factor proportions theorem.

# Regional Models of World Trade

Predöhl, Andreas. *Das Ende der Weltwirtschaftskrise — Eine Einführung in die Probleme der Weltwirtschaft.* Reinbek bei Hamburg: Rowohlt, 1962.

An introduction to Predöhl's concept of the world economy. This concept is dynamic and spatial. Each phase in the development of the world economy is characterized by its own unique commercial and financial institutions and, related to that, its own regional structure comprised of core areas and periphery.

____. *Aussenwirtschaft.* 2nd ed. Göttingen: Vandenhoeck und Ruprecht, 1971.

A textbook which elaborates upon the evolution of the modern world economy, its institutions, its technology, and its spatial organization into core areas and periphery. Current issues of commercial and monetary policies are related to this spatial organization.

Harborth, Hans-Jürgen. *Neue Industriezentren an der weltwirtschaftlichen Peripherie.* Hamburg: Hoffmann und Campe for the Deutsche Übersee-Institut, 1967.

Where are new core areas likely to evolve? This monograph identifies symptoms of core area growth and examines China, India, Australia, South Africa, and Brazil — as well as Japan — for those symptoms.

____. "On the Role of Developing Countries in a Multicentric World Economy." *Economics — A Biannual Collection of Recent German Contributions to the Field of Economic Science,* Vol. 5 (1972), pp. 68-83.

The purpose of global economic development cannot be the spreading of manufacturing industries over the entire earth. The modern world economy is necessarily comprised of core areas and periphery. Only populous, densely settled regions afford realistic opportunities for core area growth.

Platt, Robert S. *Latin America — Countrysides and United Regions.* New York: McGraw-Hill, 1942.

The concluding chapter relates Latin America to the global pattern of economic and political organization. It demonstrates how the transport and communication networks of peripheral regions are arranged to facilitate core-periphery rather than intraperiphery trade. More generally the book provides close-up views of rural peripheral economies — commercial and subsistence — and their spatial relationships, or lack thereof.

# Industrial Location, Linkage, and Growth

Weber, Alfred. *Theory of the Location of Industries.* Translated by Carl J. Friedrich. Chicago: University of Chicago Press, 1929.

Weber's theory of the location of manufacturing provides a useful framework for classifying industries by their locational characteristics. As a guide for location decisions, however, it is inadequate, because it assumes that manufacturers seek to minimize their costs rather than maximize their profits.

Leontief, Wassily. *Input-Output Economics.* New York: Oxford University Press, 1966.

Input-output analysis describes and projects the linkages among branches of an economy. The branches may be individual firms, more or less minutely defined industries, broadly defined economic sectors, or regional units of one size or another. This anthology by the pioneer of input-output analysis exemplifies and explains how it is used in the solution of specific problems.

Hoover, Edgar M. *An Introduction to Regional Economics.* New York: Alfred A. Knopf, 1971.

A modern textbook with numerous illustrations and insights on the process of regional growth and development.

Estall, Robert C., and Buchanan, Robert Ogilvie. *Industrial Activity and Economic Geography — A Study of the Forces Behind the Geographical Location of Productive Activity in Manufacturing Industry.* Rev. ed. London: Hutchinson University Library, 1966.

A general treatise on the forces affecting the location of manufacturing industries, including a good chapter on the many forms of government intervention.

Alexandersson, Gunnar. *Geography of Manufacturing.* Englewood Cliffs, New Jersey: Prentice-Hall, 1967.

A description and analysis of the distribution and migration of specific manufacturing industries.

Platt, Robert S. "A Classification of Manufactures, Exemplified by Porto Rican Industries." *Annals of the Association of American Geographers*, Vol. 17 (June 1927), pp. 79-91.

Presents a classification of manufacturing industries by their spatial relationships, as follows: Group I: those using local (Puerto Rican) materials, catering to foreign (non-Puerto Rican) markets; Group II: those using foreign materials, catering to local markets; Group III: those using local materials, catering to local markets; and Group IV: those using foreign materials, catering to foreign markets. Conceptually Platt's classification differs from my classification of peripheral industries by their dominant location factors. In practice, however, applied to Puerto Rico in the 1920s, there happens to be a perfect correspondence: the industries in Group I are all raw material-oriented, those in Groups II and III are oriented toward markets for finished goods other than capital goods for the manufacturing sector, and those in Group IV are dependent on low-wage labor.

Harris, Chauncy D. "The Market as a Factor in the Localization of Industry in the United States." *Annals of the Association of American Geographers*, Vol. 44 (December 1954), pp. 315-348.

Accessibility to national or regional (as opposed to local) markets is a powerful attraction to many manufacturing industries. The core area is the region of relatively greatest market potential as well as market accessibility.

Ullman, Edward L. "Regional Development and the Geography of Concentration." *Papers and Proceedings of the Regional Science Association*, Vol. 4 (1958), pp. 179-198.

Demonstrates that the North' American core area contains a remarkable concentration of population, manufacturing, and high-order services.

____. *American Commodity Flow — A Geographical Interpretation of Rail and Water Traffic Based on Principles of Spatial Interchange*. Seattle: University of Washington Press, 1957.

This study strikingly demonstrates the adaptation of the United States transport system to the requirements of intracore, core-periphery, and intraperiphery trade. When interpreting the numerous cartographic illustrations, it must be kept in mind that they exhibit shipments in terms of tonnages, not in terms of dollar values.

Beyers, William B. "Growth Centers and Interindustry Linkages." *Proceedings of the Association of American Geographers*, Vol. 5 (1973), pp. 18-21.

An interregional input-output analysis demonstrates that the industries of the Seattle-Tacoma-Everett region are less firmly linked with each other than with industries beyond that region. The author suggests that this is attributable to the small size of that region, and that growth stimuli through backward and forward linkages are probably more effective on a national scale. (The regional theory of world trade, on the other hand, suggests that the size of the Seattle-Tacoma-Everett region is less significant than the fact that it is a peripheral manufacturing center. An equally large region with more core industries would exhibit substantially closer interindustry linkages.)

Baldwin, George B. "Industrialization: A Standard Pattern." *Finance and Development*, Vol. 3 (December 1966), pp. 274-282.

Explains the process of industrial growth through industrial linkages. Written in plain language and illustrated with pertinent examples from developing countries.

Fuchs, Victor R. *Changes in the Location of Manufacturing in the United States since 1929.* New Haven: Yale University Press, 1962.

In the United States the secular trend has been a dispersal of manufacturing from the northeastern core area to the periphery and to incipient core areas in southern California and eastern Texas. This book presents a comprehensive analysis of this trend during the period 1929 to 1954.

Manners, Gerald. "Regional Protection: A Factor in Economic Geography." *Economic Geography*, Vol. 38 (April 1962), pp. 122-129.

A critical discussion of government policies to effect a geographical dispersal of manufacturing industries within France, the United Kingdom, and Ireland.

## The Impact of Technology on Industrial Location and the Patterns of Trade

Vernon, Raymond. "International Investment and International Trade in the Product Cycle." *Quarterly Journal of*

*Economics*, Vol. 80 (May 1966), pp. 190-207.

The United States market, characterized by high income levels and high unit labor costs, provides special incentives to develop labor saving devices. As a new product passes through its life cycle, the market for the product expands at home and abroad. The production process becomes increasingly mechanized. Competitors enter the field, and the price of the product declines. At this stage, American firms are likely to invest in production facilities abroad. In the final stage of the cycle, countries with low unit labor costs may offer competitive advantages as a production location, and the United States may become a net importer of the product.

Wells, Louis T., Jr., ed. *The Product Life Cycle and International Trade.* Boston: Harvard University, Graduate School of Business Administration, Division of Research, 1972.

The introductory essay by the editor presents a summary of the product life cycle theory and compares it with other explanations of trade patterns. Other essays exemplify the range of the theory's applications.

Balassa, Bela. "Tariff Reductions and Trade in Manufactures among the Industrial Countries." *American Economic Review*, Vol. 56 (June 1966), pp. 466-473.

Demonstrates that intracore trade in manufactured goods consists largely of an exchange of similar or identical products, and attributes this to intraindustry — as distinguished from interindustry — specialization.

Grubel, Herbert G., and Lloyd, P. J. *Intra-Industry Trade — The Theory and Measurement of International Trade in Differentiated Products.* New York: John Wiley and Sons, 1975.

A major study of the exchange of similar or identical commodities in international trade. Presents statistical evidence of such trade and a comprehensive analysis of its economic bases. The findings pertain mostly to intracore and intercore trade.

## The Imbalance of Core Areas and Periphery

Levin, Jonathan V. *The Export Economies — Their Pattern of Development in Historical Perspective.* Cambridge, Massachusetts: Harvard University Press, 1960.

An excellent introduction to the peripheral economies. The focus is on the evolution of their economic, social, and political institutions.

[Haberler, Gottfried; Campos, Roberto de Oliveira; Meade, James; and Tinbergen, Jan.] *Trends in International Trade — Report by a Panel of Experts.* Geneva: Contracting Parties to the General Agreement on Tariffs and Trade, 1958.

The chief concern is with the stagnation of core-periphery trade. Although the report pertains to the institutional setting of the late 1950s, it is still relevant to the contemporary scene.

Nurkse, Ragnar. *Patterns of Trade and Development.* Wicksell Lectures 1959. Stockholm: Almqvist and Wiksell, 1959. Reprinted in Nurkse, Ragnar. *Problems of Capital Formation in Underdeveloped Countries and Patterns of Trade and Development,* pp. 163-227. New York: Oxford University Press, 1967.

Three relationships between international trade and economic development are examined: (1) In the nineteenth century exports of primary products provided the decisive "engine of growth" for the developing countries; but in the twentieth century only the oil exporting countries find rapidly expanding markets for their products. (2) A potential alternative to developing countries might be the fostering of manufacturing industries producing consumer goods for export to the developed countries; but this is likely to be frustrated by protectionism in the developed countries. (3) The most promising alternative to many developing countries is continued reliance on exports of primary products in exchange for imports of capital goods, and the fostering of manufacturing industries catering to the domestic market.

Payer, Cheryl, ed. *Commodity Trade of the Third World.* New York: John Wiley and Son, 1975.

A collection of essays on the production and international marketing of oil, copper, zinc, cereals, sugar, bananas, and coffee. The concluding essay by the editor is a sophisticated, nonstatistical examination of the presumed relationship between the widespread poverty in underdeveloped countries and the prices of their major export commodities.

[Prebisch, Raul.] *The Economic Development of Latin America and Its Principal Problems.* Lake Success, New York: United Nations Department of Economic Affairs for the United Nations Economic Commission for Latin America, 1950.

The unsatisfactory growth of the Latin American economies is attributed to the self-serving economic policies of the entrepreneurs, labor unions, and government of the United States. (This document set the stage for many subsequent assaults by United Nations agencies upon the economic policies of the United States and the core countries of Western Europe.)

Viner, Jacob. *International Trade and Economic Development — Lectures Delivered at the National University of Brazil.* Glencoe, Illinois: Free Press, 1952.

An eloquent defense of classical and neo-classical trade theory against the charge that it rationalizes an unjust division of labor between core and peripheral countries. All countries have much to gain from a multilateral reduction of trade barriers.

Haberler, Gottfried. *International Trade and Economic Development.* National Bank of Egypt, Fiftieth Anniversary Commemoration Lectures. Cairo: National Bank of Egypt, 1959.

A broad attack upon the widely held notion that international trade is inimical to the interests of developing countries and an instrument of exploitation by the rich.

## Territorial Units: Nations, Customs Unions, and the Multinational Enterprise

Röpke, Wilhelm. *International Economic Disintegration.* Appendix by Alexander Rüstow. New York: Macmillan and Co., 1942.

The disintegration of the world economy is attributed to a deep-rooted social-political disintegration. It is argued that the *laissez faire* policies of the nineteenth century have failed to provide for social justice and strong, impartial governments. Thus, the liberal world order which had rested on an "undisputed code of moral norms and principles of behaviour" in the social, economic, political, and military spheres has yielded to national economic planning and an irrational, arbitrary conduct of foreign relations.

[Hilgerdt, Folke.] *The Network of World Trade.* League of Nations Publication; II, Economic and Financial. Geneva: League of Nations, Economic Intelligence Service, 1942.

A study of the volume, commodity composition, and direction of international trade. It focuses on the development of a multilateral system of trade in the latter part of the nineteenth century and the disintegration of that system since 1931.

Viner, Jacob. "Memorandum on the Technique of Present-Day Protectionism." In *Separate Memoranda on the Improvement of Commercial Relations between Nations and the Problem of Monetary Stabilization*, pp. 58-79. Paris: Joint Committee, Carnegie Endowment and International Chamber of Commerce, 1936. Reprinted in Viner, Jacob. *International Economics*, pp. 161-177. Glencoe, Illinois: Free Press, 1951.

Deals with the difficulties of measuring accurately the effects of tariffs on the volume of trade, on the economy of the country imposing the tariffs, and on the economies of its actual or potential trade partners. In many cases tariffs are a minor element in the restriction of international trade. Since the 1930s trade has been hampered also by import quotas, instable exchange rates, and restrictions on capital movements.

Hirschman, Albert O. *National Power and the Structure of Foreign Trade*. Berkeley: University of California Press, 1945.

Discusses the purposes and methods of economic warfare among nations, and substantiates the existence of such warfare during the 1930s with statistical evidence. Nazi Germany is presented as the chief villain. But, as the author has pointed out, "power elements . . . are potentially inherent in such 'harmless' trade relations as have always taken place, e.g., between big and small, rich and poor, agricultural and industrial countries — relations which could be fully in accord with the principles taught by the theory of international trade. Political power may only be latent in such commercial relations. But so long as war remains a possibility and so long as the sovereign nation can interrupt trade with any country at its own will, the contest for more national power permeates trade relations, and foreign trade provides an opportunity for power which it will be tempting to seize." (Many of the charges which Hirschman has leveled against Nazi Germany have since been directed against nations usually inclined toward more liberal trade policies, such as the United Kingdom and the United States.)

Michaely, Michael. *Concentration in International Trade* Amsterdam: North-Holland Publishing Company, 1967.

An international comparison of specialization in the commodity structure of exports and imports, specialization in trade partners, and the relative dominance of countries as exporters or importers in the world market. Explains the findings and explores their implications for exchange rate policies, price fluctuations, and economic development.

Tamedly, Elisabeth L. *Socialism and International Economic Order.* Caldwell, Idaho: Caxton Printers, 1969.

A comprehensive study of the impact of socialist ideology and institutions on the foreign trade of socialist countries. An outstanding book on a much belabored topic.

Viner, Jacob. *The Customs Union Issue.* New York: Carnegie Endowment for International Peace, 1950.

A comprehensive and critical examination of the purposes for which customs unions have been proposed and of their economic and political effects. It is argued that customs unions are incompatible in principle with the most-favored-nation clause of commercial treaties, and that by economic and administrative standards they are inferior to universal free trade. Objective criteria are proposed by which to evaluate the economic impact of customs unions on the member nations and on the rest of the world. The discussion is garnished with much historical evidence.

Krauss, Melvyn B. "Recent Developments in Customs Union Theory: An Interpretative Survey." *Journal of Economic Literature,* Vol. 10 (June 1972), pp. 413-436.

Viner's pioneer analysis of the economic effects of customs unions has been qualified and amplified in the subsequent literature. But, judging from this review, it does not appear that a general theory of customs unions has evolved. (To specify the objectives of customs unions generally in terms susceptible to economic analysis seems a formidable task. Consider, for instance, the different objectives of the EC and LAFTA, the conflicting objectives of France and the United Kingdom within the EC, and the changing objectives of France as just one member of the EC.)

Müller-Armack, Alfred. "Fragen der europäischen Integration." In *Wirtschaftsfragen der Freien Welt,* 2nd ed., edited by Erwin von Beckerath, Fritz W. Meyer, and Alfred Müller-Armack, pp. 531-540. Frankfurt am Main: Fritz Knapp, 1957.

When the European Economic Community was still in its formative stage, Müller-Armack argued that the creation of a customs union would fail to meet the more basic need for cooperation in fiscal and social policies and, worse yet, would tend to make such cooperation more difficult in the future. Subsequent events have borne him out.

Harborth, Hans-Jürgen. "Anforderungen an eine revidierte Integrationstheorie für Entwicklungsländer." In *Integration der Entwicklungsländer in eine instabile Weltwirtschaft — Probleme, Chancen, Gefahren,* edited by Winfried von Urff, pp. 65-88. Berlin: Duncker und Humblot, 1976.

A policy of multinational economic integration is unrealistic if it does not involve a concept of multinational regional development. A revised theory of integration should provide answers to the following questions: (1) What combinations of national economies are suited for integrated development? (2) How shall eventual combinations of integrated economies fit into the regional structure of the world economy?

McNee, Robert B. "Centrifugal-Centripetal Forces in International Petroleum Company Regions." *Annals of the Association of American Geographers,* Vol. 51 (March 1961), pp. 124-138.

The operation of a global enterprise such as the Standard Oil Company of New Jersey involves a balancing of centripetal and centrifugal forces. The former give the enterprise coherence, direction, and flexibility; the latter represent regional and national interests. The two forces, however, do not necessarily pull in opposite directions. "The diplomatic voice of Venezuela," for instance, "is supplemented by the 'business diplomatic' voice of Jersey Standard in Washington, London, and other political capitals around the world."

Behrman, Jack N. *National Interests and the Multinational Enterprise — Tensions Among the North Atlantic Countries.* Englewood Cliffs, New Jersey: Prentice-Hall, 1970.

A discussion of the political tensions and legal problems which result from the operation of United States enterprises in Canada, Western Europe, and Australia. The governments of the host countries (where American controlled subsidiaries are located) are apprehensive about losing control over their national economies — partly because of the large size of the multinational enterprises, their flexibility in allocating capital and other resources, and their control over advanced technologies, and partly because the United States government, in applying its laws to multinational enterprises chartered in the United States, indirectly restrains their foreign affiliates in complying with the policies of their host countries. The book discusses also the measures which the governments of host countries (including Japan) have taken to confine the power of foreign controlled enterprises.

Vernon, Raymond. *Sovereignty at Bay — The Multinational Spread of U.S. Enterprise.* New York: Basic Books, 1971.

——. *The Economic and Political Consequences of Multinational Enterprise: An Anthology.* Boston: Harvard University, Graduate School of Business Administration, Division of Research, 1972.

——. *Storm over the Multinationals — The Real Issues.* Cambridge, Massachusetts: Harvard University Press, 1977.

All three books deal with the motives and strategies of multinational enterprises and with the conflicts resulting from their ability to elude effective control by national governments. They examine the geographical expansion of multinational enterprises during the post-World War II period, their role in the international transfer of technology, and their impact on employment patterns and on countries' balances of payments. The operations of multinational enterprises give rise to conflicts with the national governments of their home countries (where the parent companies are headquartered) and with the national governments of their host countries (where subsidiaries are located). Conflicts derive from the flexibility of multinational enterprises in manipulating prices for international transfers of goods and services so as to report the least profits for those affiliates which are taxed at the highest rates, and from the attempts of national governments to regulate the operations of multinational enterprises within their territories or abroad. Thus far, the diversity of interests among national governments has prevented the adoption of a coherent policy with respect to multinational enterprises.

Behrman, Jack N. *The Role of International Companies in Latin American Integration — Autos and Petrochemicals.* Lexington, Massachusetts: D.C. Heath for the Committee for Economic Development, 1972.

All members of LAFTA are intent upon obtaining a slice of the automobile and petrochemical industries. "Equity" takes precedence over efficiency. Multinational enterprises, already engaged in automobile and petrochemical production in Latin America, might be helpful in organizing these industries on a multinational basis. Latin America's national governments, however, wish to confine the activities of multinational enterprises. According to the author, LAFTA's stalemate derives largely from conflicting national interests.

## Trade Statistics

Allen, Roy G. D., and Ely, J. Edward, eds. *International Trade*

*Statistics.* New York: John Wiley and Sons, 1953.

Users of international trade statistics are often baffled by the lack of correspondence in the statistics of partner countries — by the fact that a commodity shipment from country A to country B is recorded differently in A's export statistics than in B's import statistics. This book explains why. It deals with the valuation of exports and imports, with the systems of general and special trade, and with the recording of trade partners. Also, it explains types of index numbers and their use in evaluating the terms of trade. A very useful manual.

*International Trade Statistics — Concepts and Definitions.* Statistical Papers Series M, No. 52. New York: United Nations Statistical Office, 1970.

Sets forth the recommendations of the United Nations Statistical Office as to the coverage and definition of international trade statistics.

*Standard International Trade Classification, Revised.* Statistical Papers Series M, No. 34. New York: United Nations Statistical Office, 1961.

Defines Sections, Divisions, Groups, Subgroups, and Items of the Revised SITC; and relates the Revised SITC to the original SITC (which had been in use in the 1950s) and to the Brussels Tariff Nomenclature. An appendix relates the Brussels Tariff Nomenclature to the Revised SITC.

*Classification of Commodities by Industrial Origin — Relationship of the Standard International Trade Classification to the International Standard Industrial Classification.* Statistical Papers Series M, No. 43. New York: United Nations Statistical Office, 1966.

Part I relates the Revised SITC to the ISIC, and Part II relates the ISIC to the Revised SITC. Provides a link between commodities entering international trade and the industries from which they normally flow. But no attempt is made to estimate the proportions which separate industrial activities contribute to the value of commodities, as might be undertaken through input-output analysis.

*Yearbook of International Trade Statistics,* Vol. I: *Trade by Country,* Vol. II: *Trade by Commodity — Commodity Matrix Tables.* New York: United Nations Statistical Office, annual.

Volume I contains the following information by countries: imports and exports by major trade partners; imports and exports by commodities according to the SITC; and trends in the current value, quantum index, and unit value index of imports and exports. Volume I also contains summary tables of world imports and exports; matrix tables, by commodity classes, showing the flow of trade among groups of countries; and statistics on trends in price and quantum indices, by commodity classes. Volume II presents two sets of tables: one shows, by commodities, the majcr importing and exporting countries; and the other set presents, likew.se by commodities, matrix tables of the flow of trade from major exporting to major importing countries.

*Commodity Trade Statistics.* Statistical Papers Series D. New York: United Nations Statistical Office, in frequent installments.

Each installment covers the trade of one or several countries for a calendar year or shorter period (January to March, January to June, or January to September). For each country, the data show imports and exports by commodities according to origin or destination, respectively. The publication covers the trade of all the major market economies and of some smaller countries as well.

*Direction of Trade.* Washington, D.C.: International Monetary Fund, annual issues.

Reports for countries and for groups of countries the destination of exports and the origin of imports. Data for the centrally planned economies are derived from the trade statistics of the market economies; they exclude, therefore, trade among the centrally planned economies.

*International Financial Statistics.* Washington, D.C.: International Monetary Fund, monthly.

The most up-to-date report on the market economies. Covers data on foreign trade and on a wide range of related topics such as commodity prices, exchange rates, balance of payments, and national accounts. All issues contain tables by subjects and tables by countries. Some issues present twenty or twenty-five year series of internationally comparable data.

# INDEX

Intracore trade, 38, 40-44
Intraperiphery trade, 39-40, 64-65, 72-73

Jürgensen, Harald, 40n

Kindleberger, Charles P., 54n, 69-70
Kostinsky, Barry L., 26n
Krauss, Melvyn, B., 80

LAFTA (Latin American Free Trade Association): purpose and failure, 64-66; same type of commodity exchange with the United Kingdom, 42-44
Leontief, Wassily, 70-71, 73
Levin, Jonathan V., 76-77
Linder, Staffan Burenstam, 41n, 54n
Lloyd, P. J., 41n, 76
Lösch, August, 14n
Lowell, James Russell, 50

McNee, Robert B., 81
Manners, Gerald, 17n, 75
Manufactured goods traded by core and peripheral countries, 31-35
Maritano, Nino, 65n
Meade, James, 77
Michaely, Michael, 79-80
Minhas, Bagicha Singh, 71
Morawetz, David, 65n
Müller-Armack, Alfred, 80
Multicentric world economy, 10 and passim

Nurkse, Ragnar, 50n, 77

Ohlin, Bertil, 2-7, 40n, 70

Payer, Cheryl, 77
Pedersen, Poul Ove, 66n-67n

Peripheral industries: defined, 15; related to exports of peripheral countries, 35; stimulate growth of core industries, 55-57; classified by their spatial relationships, 74
Periphery: defined, 9, 11-12; and underdevelopment, 48-55
Platt, Robert S., 72-73, 74
Plaza, Galo, 64n
Prebish, Raul, 77-78
Predöhl, Andreas, 9n, 11n, 40n, 63n, 72
Product life cycle theory, 16-17, 75-76

Raw materials defined, 13
Regionalization and its relevant context, 10, 62-63
Relative price, 2
Ricardo, David, 39
Röpke, Wilhelm, 78

Same type of commodity exchange, 6-7, 40-44; defined, 42, 44
Samuelson, Paul A., 4n, 70
Scargill, David Ian, 23n
SITC (Standard International Trade Classification), 31, 36, 42-44, 83-84
Smith, Adam, 39
Stöhr, Walter, 66n-67n

Tamedly, Elisabeth L., 19n, 21n, 80
Tariffs. See Import restrictions
Tinbergen, Jan, 77

Ullman, Edward L., 16n, 20n, 74
Unicentric world economy, 9

Vernon, Raymond, 17n, 75-76, 82
Viner, Jacob, 5n, 71-72, 78, 79, 80

Weber, Alfred, 13-14, 61-62, 73
Wells, Louis T., Jr., 17n, 76
Wilczynski, Jozef, 21n

86